北京风景
BEIJING CITYSCAPES

外文出版社
FOREIGN LANGUAGES PRESS

前 言

北京是闻名于世的历史文化名城，有着3000多年的历史，在这漫长的历史过程中，北京从一个原始聚落发育成为方国，诸侯领地的中心，进而成为封建国家北京地区的重镇，并上升为全国首都的显赫地位，进入世界著名大都市的行列，其间线索连贯、内涵丰富。至今，我们仍可以看到700年前元大都城市规划的街道布局，这在世界上是很少见的。

北京城作为都城始于辽（公元938年）称为南京，金朝继起，扩建为中都。元代忽必烈于中都东北郊建大都（汗八里），成为具有世界意义的大都会。而明、清两代主要是改建宫城、皇城，对原大都的街道规划未作改变。北京作为都城的位置选择，是地利、人和、经济、政治、军事等全方位的考虑和需要。它有力地促进了中国各民族的交流与融合，使我国多民族统一的国家得以发展和巩固。

北京地区文物古迹十分丰富，其中周口店北京人遗址、明清皇宫、长城、天坛、颐和园、明清皇家陵寝6项被列入世界文化遗产名录；60余项被列为全国重点文物保护单位，234项被列为市级文物保护单位；被列入区县级的文物保护单位更是多达700余项。近年，又确定了25片历史文化保护街区。遍布北京城内外的文物古迹，是中华民族悠久历史和灿烂文明的物质体现和光辉见证，使北京无愧于世界历史文化名城的称号。

今天的北京，正在高速地向现代化、国际性大都市发展，高速路、商业区、办公大楼、饭店、宾馆、开发区、住宅区……使北京的面貌每时每刻都在变化。但是，北京的魅力依然与它特有的历史文化传统紧密相连，并将随着历史前进的脚步得到更广更深的发扬。

Foreword（英文）

A famous city of both cultural and historic importance, Beijing has a history of over 3,000 years. From a primitive community to a political center of feudal states and then the capital of the entire nation and long a major international metropolis, Beijing has walked a splendid road. Here, we can still find well-designed streets dating back to the Yuan Dynasty 700 years ago, and this is rare in any other city in the world.

Beijing was first designated a capital city during the Liao Dynasty (916-1125) when it was named South Capital. After the Jin Dynasty (1115-1234) took over the city, it was expanded and named Central Capital. Later, Kublai Khan of the Yuan Dynasty (1271-1368) built Dadu in the northeastern suburbs of Central Capital, which then became an international metropolis. During the Ming (1368-1644) and Qing (1644-1911) dynasties, the rulers reconstructed and expanded the imperial palaces and other parts of the city, without altering the framework of streets of the former Dadu. Throughout history Beijing has served as the capital of China several times, due to an overall consideration of geographical, personnel, economic, political and military factors. It has made great contributions to the unity of China's different ethnic groups and the unification of the Chinese nation.

Beijing boasts a wealth of cultural relics, of which the Peking Man Site at Zhoukoudian, the Imperial Palaces of the Ming and Qing dynasties, the Great Wall, the Temple of Heaven, the Summer Palace and the Imperial Tombs of the Ming and Qing dynasties have been put on the World Cultural Heritage list. In addition, over 60 local historical and cultural relics are under special national protection, 234 under municipal-level protection and more than 700 under district or county-level protection. In recent years, the city has designated 25 street blocks of historical significance. The cultural heritage sites scattered around Beijing are witnesses to the splendid history and brilliant civilization of the Chinese nation, and make Beijing a world-famous metropolis of historical and cultural importance.

Today Beijing is busily making itself a modern and international metropolis. Newly built expressways, commercial districts, office buildings, restaurants, hotels, residential neighborhoods and development zones change the city's landscape every day. Even so, the charm of Beijing still lies in its ancient and profound traditions, based on which the city is moving forward.

前書き （日文）

　北京は世界的に有名な歴史と文化の名城である。その発展には3000年の長い歴史をたどってきた。最初は原始的な集落から、方国、諸侯国領地の中心として発展し、そして封建国家、北京地域の重鎮、最後は今日のような中国の首都、世界でも著名な大都会に発展してきた。その間、歴史を中断したことがなく、内容もきわめて豊富である。この点については、今日に至ってよく保たれている700年前の元（げん）の「大都」遺跡を見てもわかる。

　北京の都城としての歴史は遼（西暦938年）から始まり、そのときは南京と称された。金はこれに継いで中都と呼んだ。元のフビライが中都東北郊外に建てた大都（汗八里）は、当時でも世界的な意義がある大都会である。明、清両代は皇城に対して改築したことはあるが、旧大都の町計画に対して変えることはしなかった。北京を都城に選んだ原因は主に「地の利」と「人の和」、および経済、政治と軍事の需要など全範囲にわたって考えた結果である。これにより中国の各民族の交流と融合は力強く促され、中国も多民族の統一国家として発展を遂げて強固された。

　北京地域の文化財はきわめて豊富である。このうちの周口店の北京原人遺跡、明・清時代の皇居、万里の長城、天壇、頤和園、明・清時代の皇室陵墓などの6つは国連ユネスコによって世界文化遺産として登録されたものである。ほかにまた60以上の国重点文化財、234の市重点文化財がある。区・県級に指定された文化財はなおさら700以上に及んでいる。ここ数年にはまた25の市街を歴史文化保護区に指定している。市の所々にあるこれらの文化財は、中華民族の燦爛たる歴史と文明の活きた証人である。北京はこれらの文化財により「世界の歴史と文化の名城」の称号に輝いている。

　今日の北京は現代化、国際化を目指して急速的に発展している。高速道路、ビジネス町、オフィスビル、ホテル、開発区、住宅団地などは次々と建設され、刻一刻北京の姿を変えている。にもかかわらず、北京の古い歴史と伝統は失っていないばかりか、歴史の発展とともにより輝かしさを放すようになっている。

서언 （韓文）

　베이징은 세계에서 유명한 역사문화명성이며 3000여년의 역사를 가지고 있다. 베이징은 원시부락에서 제후국, 제후영토의 중심지, 봉건국가 베이징 지역의 중요한 요충지로 발전되었다. 현재 베이징은 중국 수도라는 혁혁한 지위로 부상되었으며 세계에서 유명한 대도시로 발전하였다. 지금까지도 우리가 여전히 700년전의 원나라 도시의 거리배치 흔적을 찾아 볼 수 있는 것은 세계에서도 아주 희소한 것이다.

　베이징성이 도읍으로 되기 시작한 것은 요나라(938년) 시기로 당시는 남경(南京)이라고 불렸고 금나라시기에는 증축하여 중도(中都)라고 불렸다. 원나라의 쿠빌라이칸 (忽必裂汗)은 중도를 동북방향으로 증축하고 대도(大都)라고 개칭하였으며 세계적으로 영향력이 있는 대도시로 발전하게 하였다. 명·청나라 후에는 주요하게 궁성, 황성 등을 개건하고 원래의 거리배치에 대해서는 고친 것이 거의 없는데 당시 베이징의 지리, 인화(人和), 경제, 정치, 군사 등 여러 요소를 감안하여 도읍성의 위치를 정한 것이다. 이것은 중화 여러 민족의 교류와 융합을 적극적으로 추진시켰으며 중국의 다민족통일의 국가로 발전하는 것을 공고히 하였다.

　베이징지역은 문화유적이 아주 풍부하다. 그 중 저우커우뎬(周口店) 베이징인 유적, 명·청나라 황궁, 장성(長城), 톈탄(天壇), 이허위안, 명·청나라 황가릉원(皇家陵園) 여섯 가지 유적은 이미 세계문화유산 명록에 기록되었으며 60여 가지 중국의 중요한 문화재로 지정되었다. 또 234여 가지는 이미 시급 문화자료로 지정되었고, 구·현급에 지정된 문화자료는 700여 가지에 달한다. 최근 몇년간 또 25개의 역사문화보호거리구역을 지정하였다. 베이징의 문화유적은 중화민족의 유구한 역사와 찬란한 문명의 물질적 표현이고 그 훌륭함의 증거일 뿐만 아니라 베이징으로 하여금 명실공히 세계역사문화명성으로 모자람이 없게 하였다.

　오늘의 베이징은 고속으로 국제적 대도시로 발전하고 있으며 고속도로, 상업구, 오피스텔, 호텔, 식당, 개발구, 주민구 등 시설들은 베이징을 현대화 도시로 부상시키고 있다. 하지만 베이징의 매력은 여전히 그가 지니고 있는 역사문화전통과 밀접히 연결되어 있다. 현재 베이징은 역사의 발전과 함께 광범하고 깊은 발전을 가져오고 있다.

Premessa （意大利文）

　Pechino, famosa città culturale e oggi grande metropoli internazionale, vanta oltre 3.000 anni di storia nel corso della quale vi vissero delle comunità neolitiche, e divenne via via un'importante contea dell'epoca feudale.

　Pechino fu prima la capitale della dinastia Liao e fu in seguito chiamata Nanjing (capitale del sud). La dinastia Jin promosse la riedificazione su grande scala della capitale a cui diede nome di Zhongdu. Il fondatore della dinastia Yuan, Kublai Khan, dispose la costruzione della nuova capitale Dadu nella periferia nord-orientale di Zhongdu, facendola diventare una metropoli di stampo internazionale. Durante le dinastie Ming e Qing, Pechino fu ampliata e rinnovata con l'edificazione di grandi palazzi, fino a renderla una grande città imperiale. La struttura urbana originaria delle strade e delle vie della città di Dadu furono conservate e la scelta di fare di Pechino la capitale fu presa grazie alla sua posizione geografica favorevole, che favoriva la vita degli esseri umani, la crescita economica, la politica e per la sua posizione strategica, che favoriva lo scambio e la convivenza fra i diversi gruppi etnici esistenti in Cina.

　I monumenti storici nella zona di Pechino sono numerosi; fra essi si annoverano il Museo dell'*Homo Pekinensis*, la Città Proibita, la Grande Muraglia, il Tempio del Cielo, il Palazzo d'Estate e le tombe degli imperatori delle dinastie Ming e Qing, tutti divenuti parte della lista dei patrimoni culturali mondiali; essa racchiude al suo interno inoltre più di 60 monumenti storici tenuti sotto la protezione statale, 234 monumenti sotto la prottezione della municipalità e altri 700 monumenti tenuti sotto la protezione distrettuale.

　Negli ultimi anni, sono state istituite 25 aree e vie sotto la protezione della città. I monumenti presenti nella capitale costituiscono le testimonianze della lunga storia, della civiltà e dello splendore della nazione cinese.

　Oggi, Pechino sta attraversando un'importante fase di grande sviluppo, lungo il cammino della modernizzazione. Le autostrade, le sue aree commerciali, gli alti edifici moderni della città, i grandi hotel, le sue zone di sviluppo e aree residenziali continuano a trasformarsi ininterrottamente.

Avant-propos （法文）

Beijing, célèbre ville de culture et d'histoire connue du monde entier, a une histoire de plus de 3 000 ans. Au cours de cette longue période, Beijing qui était à l'origine un village primitif est devenu peu à peu une contrée prospère, le centre feudataire, une importante ville dans la région de Beijing sous le régime monarchique et enfin, la capitale de toute la Chine. Aujourd'hui, la ville de Beijing a déjà pris rang parmi les grandes fameuses métropoles du monde. De nos jours encore, le plan urbain et la disposition des rues de la ville de Dadu, fondée sous la dynastie des Yuan il y a 700 ans, s'y distinguent nettement, ce qui est rarement vu au monde.

Beijing devint pour la première fois la capitale sous la dynastie des Liao (916 – 1125), dénommée Nanjing (capitale du sud). Puis, les Jin (1115 – 1234) y installèrent également leur capitale, connue sous le nom de Zhongdu. Sous les Yuan (1271 – 1368), Koubilaï Khan fit construire Dadu (Khanbali) aux environs nord-est de Zhongdu, qui était alors une grande métropole à l'échelle mondiale. Sous les Ming (1368 – 1644) et les Qing (1644 – 1911), la Cité interdite fut reconstruite, mais la disposition des rues de Dadu restait inchangée. C'est compte tenu de tous les facteurs agissants que Beijing fut choisi comme capitale, tels que sa position géographique favorable, la concorde qui régnait parmi les hommes, sa situation économique, politique et militaire ainsi que les besoins réels. En tant que capitale de plusieurs dynasties, Beijing joua un rôle capital pour intensifier les échanges entre les différentes ethnies et leur fusion, et contribua grandement au développement et à la consolidation de la Chine, Etat multinational et unifié.

La région de Beijing est riche en patrimoine culturel et en monuments historiques dont le Site de l'Homme de Beijing de Zhoukoudian, le Palais impérial des Ming et des Qing, la Grande Muraille, le Temple du Ciel, le Palais d'Eté et les nécropoles impériales des Ming et des Qing ont été inscrits sur la Liste du Patrimoine mondial, une soixantaine de sites ont été placés sous la protection de l'Etat comme monuments historiques d'importance nationale, 234 sont protégés par la municipalité de Beijing et plus de 700 protégés par les gouvernements à l'échelon du district ou de l'arrondissement. Ces dernières années, 25 quartiers résidentiels ont été désignés comme sites protégés d'intérêt culturel et historique. Les sites célèbres et les monuments historiques qui parsèment la ville de Beijing sont les témoins de la longue histoire et de la brillante civilisation ancienne de la nation chinoise, la rendant digne d'être une ville de culture et d'histoire d'une réputation mondiale.

Aujourd'hui, Beijing se développe à une vitesse prodigieuse pour devenir une grande métropole internationale. Avec l'apparition sans cesse des nouvelles artères, des quartiers commerciaux, des immeubles de bureaux, des restaurants, des grands hôtels, des zones de développement économique et des quartiers résidentiels, Beijing change d'aspect à tout moment. Pourtant, le charme de Beijing réside toujours dans ses traditions culturelles propres à elle et avec le développement incessant de l'histoire, cette ville deviendra encore de plus en plus attrayante.

Vorwort （德文）

Beijing, die Hauptstadt der Volksrepublik China, ist eine weltbekannte historische Kulturstadt und hat eine Geschichte von mehr als 3000 Jahren. Im Laufe der Jahrhunderte entwickelte sich Beijing von einer Siedlung der Urgesellschaft zum Zentrum des Fürstenstaates Yan, dan zu einer wichtigen Stadt der Feudalgesellschaft und schließlich der Hauptstadt des Landes sowie der Weltmetropole. Heute gibt es hier noch viele 700 Jahre alte Straßen aus der Yuan-Dynastie.

Als die Hauptstadt begann Beijing während der Liao-Dynastie (916—1125) und trug den Namen Nanjing. Nach der Gründung der Jin-Dynastie (1115—1234) diente Beijing als die Hauptstadt der Monarchie mit dem Namen Zhongdu. Unter der Herrschaft des Yuan-Kaisers Kubilai wurde im nordöstlichen Vorort von Zhongdu die Khauptstadt der Yuan-Dynastie mit dem Namen Dadu (in der mongolischen Sprache Khanbali genannt). Damals gehörte Dadu zu einer Weltmetropole. Während der Zeit der Ming- und Qing-Dynastie (1644—1911) wurden die Palaststadt und die Kaiserstadt von Dadu umgebaut. Die ehemaligen Straßen von Dadu wurden aber nicht verändert. Beijing wurde als Hauptstadt des Landes gewählt, nicht nur wegen seiner günstigen geologischen Lage, sondern auch wegen seiner wirtschaftlich, politisch und militärisch wichtigen Bedeutung. Dies war sehr günstig für den Austausch und die Harmonie aller Nationalitäten des Landes und für die Entwicklung und Konsolidierung Chinas als ein einheitlicher Nationalitätenstaat.

Als eine alte Kulturstadt verfügt Beijing über reiche Kulturdenkmäler, wichtige davon sind die Heimstätte des „Peking-Menschen" in Zhoukoudian, der Kaiserpalast, die Große Mauer, der Himmelstempel, der Sommerpalast und die Kaisergräber der Ming- und Qing-Dynastie (sie wurden schon in die Liste des Weltkulturerbes aufgenommen). Darüber hinaus gibt es hier über 60 Schwerpunkte des Denkmalschutzes der Staatsebene, 234 Schwerpunkte des Denkmalschutzes der Stadtsebene und mehr als 700 Schwerpunkte des Denkmalsschutzes der Bezirk- oder Kreisebene. In den letzten Jahren wurden 25 Wohnreviere Beijings unter Denkmalschutz gestellt.

Heute steht Beijing auf dem Weg der rapiden Entwicklung zu einer modernen Weltmetropole. Überall sieht man in Beijing im Bau befindliche und fertiggestellte Autobahnen, Geschäftsviertel, Bürogebäude, Hotels und Wohnhäuser. Aber die Charme Beijings ist mit seiner Geschichts- und Kulturtradition aufs engste verbunden.

Предисловие （俄文）

Пекин − всемирно известный исторический и культурный город. История города начиналась более 3000 лет назад. Сначала он только являлся населенным пунктом, потом стал центром владений феодалов, центральным городом в районе Пекин феодального княжества, дальше и столицей всей страны, одним из известных мегаполисов в мире. Теперь мы еще можем увидеть план столицы династии Юань, который был проектирован 700 лет назад. Это редко встречается в мире.

Пекин стал столицей при династии Ляо (в 938 г.) и переименовался в Наньцзин (южная столица). В династии Цзинь Пекин был расширен. Во время династии Юань император Хубилай сделал Пекин известным крупным городом в мире. При династиях Мин и Цин только реконструировали дворцы, не изменяя план бывшей юаньской столицы. Выбрали Пекин как столица, учитывая многие факторы, включая географический, политический, экономический, военный. Без сомнения. Пекин сильно способствует обмену китайских национальностей, развитию и укреплению многонационального Китая.

В Пекине много достопримечательностей. В том числе, Великая китайская стена, живописный парк Ихэюань, музей Гугун, Храм неба, первобытная стоянка «Пекинского синантропа» Чжоукоудянь и могилы минских и цинских императоров были занесены ЮНЕСКО в реестр объектов мирового культурного наследия. Более 60 достопримечательностей находятся под охраной государства, 234 достопримечательностей − под охраной города, более 700 − под охраной района и уезда. В последние годы 25 исторических и культурных кварталов были взяты под охраной. Исторические достопримечательности в Пекине являются материальным показанием и свидетелями длинной истории и лучезарной культуры.

Сегодняшний Пекин быстро развивается в направлении современного, мирового мегаполиса. Здесь есть высокоскоростные дороги, коммерческие районы, офисы-здания, рестораны, гостиницы, районы освоения, кварталы. Облик Пекина меняется в каждую минуту. Но его культура и традиции еще живут в каждых углах города, и развиваются со временем.

Prólogo （西文）

Beijing, ciudad histórica y cultural de fama mundial, tiene un pasado de más de 3.000 años, en los que evolucionó de sede de tribu primordial a Estado, centro del feudo de príncipes e importante punto estratégico, hasta que por fin devino capital de todo el imperio, distinguiéndose entre reconocidas metrópolis del mundo. Aún en el presente guarda la distribución de las calles establecida hace 700 haños, cuando fue capital de la dinastía Yuan, algo muy difícil de encontrar en otras urbes del planeta.

En la dinastía Liao (938), fue cuando por primera vez la ciudad se convirtió en capital del país con el nombre de Nanjing (capital del sur) y en el siguiente dominio, el de la dinastía Jin, mantuvo su papel, bautizada como Zhongdu (capital central). En el suburbio del noreste de Zhongdu, Qubilai, emperador fundador del poder mongol Yuan, ordenó construir el centro de su vasto imperio, la Gran Capital, y lo desarrolló hasta convertirlo en una metrópolis internacional. En las dinastías posteriores, como Ming y Qing, aunque las ciudades Prohibida e Imperial fueron reconstruidas y modificadas, las calles de la Gran Capital lograron mantener su fisonomía original. La decisión de fundar la capital en Beijing fue tomada teniendo en cuenta su posición geográfica, económica, política y militar, además de otras condiciones y demandas en diferentes aspectos del imperio, como promover fuertemente el intercambio y la convivencia de las naciones chinas y reforzar y fomentar el Estado unificado y multinacional de China.

Beijing es muy rico por sus reliquias culturales, entre las que se incluyen 6 patrimonios culturales de la humanidad, como el Sitio del Hombre de Pekín, en Zhoukoudian, los palacios imperiales de las dinastías Ming y Qing, la Gran Muralla, el Templo del Cielo, el Palacio de Verano y los mausoleos imperiales de Ming y Qing, así como más de 60 vestigios claves del nivel estatal, 234 municipal y más de 700 de distrito. En los últimos años, 25 barrios fueron denominados históricos y culturales protegidos. Estas reliquias que se aprecian por todas partes son testigos y representación material de la larga historia y brillante civilización de la nación china y otorgaron a Beijing el título de famosa ciudad histórica y cultural.

Hoy en día, la capital china experimenta un desarrollo a alta velocidad hacia la meta de convertirse en una moderna metrópolis internacional. Las autopistas, barrios y edificios comerciales, hoteles, zonas de explotación, repartos residenciales... están modificando su imagen aceleradamente, pero la mayor atracción continúa radicando en su antigua tradición y cultura, más marcada y conocida con el avance del tiempo.

北京的世界文化遗产——长城

　　万里长城是中华民族精神的象征。从公元前7世纪的春秋战国至公元17世纪的明代末年，长城的修建延续了2000多年，在中国辽阔的土地上，长城东起辽宁的鸭绿江畔，绵延数万里，向西一直奔向甘肃的莽莽雪山。

　　长城作为军事防御的设施，证明了中华民族自古以来热爱和平、反对入侵的坚定信念和不懈追求，北京段长城主要包括八达岭长城、慕田峪长城、司马台长城等，这一部分长城的建筑形式和质量在万里长城中最有特色、保存最好，大都于明代前期修建，它们起着拱卫京师、保护皇陵的重要作用。

World Cultural Heritage Sites in Beijing: The Great Wall（英文）

The Great Wall is the spiritual symbol of the Chinese nation. The construction of the wall lasted more than 2,000 years, from the 7th century BC during the Spring and Autumn Period (770-476 BC) through the 17th century AD during the Ming Dynasty. It stretches for thousands of kilometers, from Liaoning Province's Yalu River in the east to Gansu Province's snowcapped mountains in the west.

As an ancient military fortification, the Great Wall embodies the Chinese people's love for peace and their resolution to repel foreign aggression. The main sections of the Great Wall in the Beijing area include Badaling, Mutianyu and Simatai. Mainly built during the early Ming Dynasty, these sections are the most distinctive and best-preserved parts of the entire Great Wall. In ancient times, they played an important role in defending the capital and imperial tombs.

Patrimonios culturales de la humanidad de Beijing
La Gran Muralla （西文）

Como símbolo espiritual de la nación china, la Gran Muralla partió de su extremo oriental, en la orilla del río Yalu, y terminó en el occidental, entre las montañas nevadas de la provincia de Gansu. Más de 2.000 años se invirtieron para la construcción de esta maravilla, desde el siglo VII (a.C.), la época de la Primavera y el Otoño hasta el siglo XVII (d.C.), últimos años de la dinastía Ming.

Como baluarte militar, la Gran Muralla representa la aspiración por la paz y firme resistencia del pueblo chino contra las invasiones extranjeras. En el territorio de Beijing la monumental obra cuenta con los tramos de Badaling, Mutianyu y Simatai, entre otros, que se distinguen por su arquitectura variada y construcción de calidad, además de ser reconocidos por sus típicos caracteres y buen estado de conservación. Estas partes se levantaron en general en los primeros años de la dinastía Ming y desde entonces desempeñaron un importante papel en la protección de la capital y los mausoleos imperiales.

Weltkulturerbe Beijings: Die Große Mauer （德文）

Die Große Mauer ist das Symbol des Geistes der chinesischen Nation. Der Bau der Großen Mauer dauerte mehr als 2000 Jahre, er begann in der Frühlings- und Herbstperiode und der Zeit der Streitenden Reiche (7. Jahrhundert v. Chr.) und endete in der Zeit der Ming-Dynastie (17. Jahrhundert). Dieses imposante Bauwerk nimmt im Osten am Ufer des Yalu-Flusses innerhalb der Provinz Liaoning seinen Anfang und erstreckt sich westwärts über mehrere Zehntausende km bis zum Jayu-Pass in der Provinz Gansu.

Als eine Verteidigungsanlage stellt die Große Mauer einen Beweis dafür dar, dass die chinesische Nation seit dem Altertum danach strept, den Frieden zu lieben und gegen fremde Eingriffe zu kämpfen. Von der Großen Mauer gibt es in der Umgebung Beijings heute noch mehrere Abschnitte. Die wichtigen Mauerabscbnitte befinden sich in Badaling, Mutianyu und Simatai. All diese Mauerabschnitte wurden in der Ming-Dynastie gebaut und sind heute noch gut erhalten.

베이징의 세계문화유산 - 장성 （韩文）

　만리장성은 중화민족 정신의 상징이다. 기원전 7 세기의 춘추전국시기부터 기원 17 세기 명조말년까지 장성의 수건은 2000 여년간 지속되었다. 중국의 넓은 토지에서 장성은 동쪽의 요닝성 압록강부터 서쪽으로 수만리로 뻗어 간쑤（甘肃）의 망망한 설산까지 이른다.

　군사방어시설로서 장성은 중화민족의 자고로부터 평화를 사랑하고 외래의 침입을 반대하는 확고한 신념과 끝없는 추구를 증명한다. 베이징 지역의 장성은 바다링（八達岭）장성, 무톈위（慕田峪）장성, 스마타이（司馬台）장성 등이 있는데 이 부분의 장성의 건설 형태와 품질은 만리장성 중에서 가장 특색있고, 가장 잘 보존된 것으로, 대부분 명조 전기에 수건한 것이다. 이것은 베이징을 방위하고 황능을 보호하는데 중요한 작용을 일으켰다.

北京の世界文化遺産－万里の長城 （日文）

　万里の長城は中華民族精神のシンボルである。西暦紀元前 7 世紀の春秋戦国時代から西暦 17 世紀の明の末年に至るまで、長城の築造は 2000 年も続いた。長城は東の遼寧省の鴨緑江畔にはじまり、えんえん数万里をたどって、西の甘粛省の雪山に伸びている。

　長城は軍事防御施設として築造されたものである。ここから見ても中華民族が昔から平和を愛し、断固と侵略に反対する民族であることがわかる。北京地域の長城は主に八達嶺、慕田峪、司馬台などを含む。これらの長城は建築の様式も品質も、万里の長城ではもっとも特色がある区間で、しかももっとも完全に保たれている。明代前期に築造されたこれらの長城は、都城、皇居と皇室陵墓を守るためにきわめて大きな役割を果たしていた。

La Grande Muraglia, ufficialmente riconosciuta dall'UNESCO come patrimonio culturale mondiale a Pechino （意大利文）

La Grande Muraglia lunga diecimila *li* (misura più o meno corrispondente al mezzo chilometro) è il simbolo della nazione cinese. L'opera di costruzione della Grande Muraglia durò per oltre 2000 anni a partire dal Periodo delle Primavere e degli Autunni e degli Stati Combattenti nel VII secolo a.C, fino alla fine della dinastia Ming nel XVII secolo. Attraversando da est a ovest la vasta distesa del grande territorio cinese, essa si estende dalle rive del fiume Yalu nella provincia del Liaoning a est, e si allunga verso ovest fino ai monti innevati della provincia del Gansu.

Struttura fortificata militare testimonia la volontà nella storia della Cina a mantenere la pace e la tranquillità sin dall'epoca antica. Le sezioni più note di Grande Muraglia presenti nei pressi di Pechino sono quelle di Badaling, Mutianyu e Simatai che furono edificate principalmente durante la dinastia Ming, e sono caratterizzate da uno stile architettonico particolare e dal buon stato di conservazione. La Grande Muraglia in queste aree svolse un ruolo molto importante nella difesa della capitale e dei suoi importanti palazzi imperiali.

Sites du patrimoine mondial à Beijing
La Grande Muraille （法文）

La Grande Muraille longue de 5 000 kilomètres est le symbole de l'esprit de la nation chinoise. Les travaux de construction de la Grande Muraille durèrent plus de 2 000 ans, du VIIᵉ siècle avant Jésus-Christ jusqu'au XVIIᵉ siècle, à savoir de l'époque des Printemps et Automnes et des Royaumes combattants jusqu'à la fin de la dynastie des Ming. Dans le vaste territoire de la Chine, la Grande Muraille qui part du bord du fleuve Yalu dans la province du Liaoning à l'est se dirige vers les montagnes enneigées dans la province du Gansu à l'ouest en parcourant plus de 5 000 kilomètres.

En tant qu'ouvrage de défense militaire, la Grande Muraille témoigne de la conviction inébranlable de la nation chinoise qui aime depuis toujours la paix et qui lutte contre l'invasion, et de ses efforts inlassables à cette fin. La Grande Muraille qui traverse Beijing comprend essentiellement la section de Badaling, celle de Mutianyu et celle de Simatai parmi lesquelles les parties les plus belles du point de vue de la forme architecturale et de la qualité de construction et les mieux conservées ont été bâties pour la plupart pendant les premières années des Ming. Elles jouèrent un rôle important pour défendre la capitale et protéger les tombeaux impériaux.

③ 乾隆皇帝像
A portrait of Emperor Qianlong(r. 1736-1795) of the Qing Dynasty
清・乾隆帝像
청나라 건륭제상
Portrait de l'empereur Qianlong des Qing
Bildnis des Qing-Kaisers Qian Long
Ritratto dell'imperatore Qianlong della dinastia Qing
Портрет цинского императора Цяньлун
Retrato del emperador Qianlong, de la dinastía Qing

④ 保和殿内景
Inside the Hall of Preserved Harmony
保和殿の内部風景
보화전 내부
Une vue intérieure de la Salle de l'Harmonie préservée
Innenansicht der Baohe-Halle
L'interno del Palazzo dell'Armonia Preservata
Внутри павильона Баохэдянь
Interior del Pabellón de Armonía Preservada

⑤ 乾清宫内景
Inside the Palace of Heavenly Purity
乾清宫の内部風景
건청궁 내부
Une vue intérieure du Palais de la Pureté céleste
Innenansicht des Qianqing-Palastes
L'interno del Palazzo della Purezza Celeste
Внутри павильона Цяньциндянь
Interior de la Pabellón de la Pureza Celeste

⑥ 交泰殿内景
Inside the Hall of Union and Peace
交泰殿の内部風景
교태전 내부
Une vue intérieure de la Salle de l'Union
Innenansicht der Jiaotai-Halle
L'interno del Palazzo della Grande Unione
Внутри павильона Цзяотайдянь
Interior del Pabellón de las Relaciones Celeste y Terrestre

⑦ 养心殿内景
Inside the Hall of Mental Cultivation
養心殿の内部風景
양심전 내부

Vue intérieure du Palais de la Nourriture de l'Esprit
Innenansicht der Yangxin-Halle. Früher empfang der Kaiser hier seine Minister.
L'interno del Palazzo del Perfezionamento dello Spirito in cui l'imperatore
gestiva gli affari di stato
Внутри павильона Янсиньдянь, где работал император
Interior del Pabellón Yangxin, donde por lo general el emperador trataba los
asuntos de Estado

① 堆秀山
The Hill of Accumulated Elegance
堆秀山
두이슈산
La Colline au spectacle ravissant
Das Steinwerk Duixiushan
La collina delle Eleganze Accumulate
Гора Дуйсюшань
Colina Duixiu

② 万春亭
The Pavilion of Everlasting Spring
万春亭
만춘정
Le Kiosque des Dix Mille Printemps
Der Wanchun-Pavillon
Il padiglione Wanchun
Беседка Ванчуньтин
Quiosko Wanchun

③ 故宫角楼
A watchtower of the Forbidden City
故宫の角楼   고궁의 각루
Tour d'angle du Palais impérial
Ein Eckturm
La torretta di guardia nella Città Proibita
Угловая башня Гугуна
Torre de vigilancia de la Ciudad Prohibida

青铜狮
A bronze lion
青銅獅子
청동사자
Lion de bronze
Pronzelöwe
Un leone in bronzo
Бронзовый лев
León de bronce

铜缸
A copper urn
銅カメ
구리독
Grande jarre en bronze
Wasserbehälter aus Bronze
Un recipiente di bronzo
Медный чан
Tinaja de cobre

и совершенным искусством. Они являются шедеврами в китайской архитектурной истории и частью мировых ценных наследий.

Всего 22 императора в династии Цин и Мин здесь проводили более 600 церемонии поколения Небу. Благодаря чему храм Неба обладает важным значением в изучении китайской древней политики, астрономии, календаря, философии, музыки, ритуала, живописи и т.п.

Храм Неба занимает 270 гектаров. Лес древних кипарисов, тихая окружающая среда и загадочный алтарь придают всему району необычное очарование.

Il Tempio del Cielo, patrimonio culturale mondiale a Pechino（意大利文）

Situato nella parte sudorientale di Pechino, vi è il Tempio del Cielo, un complesso che fu il luogo in cui gli imperatori delle dinastie Ming e Qing offrivano sacrifici e pregavano il Cielo per ottenere dei buoni raccolti. Costruito inizialmente nel 1420. La distribuzione degli edifici che lo compongono rappresenta la visione del mondo di allora e il concetto di Cielo e di Terra degli antichi cinesi, in cui "il Cielo è rotondo e la Terra quadrata" quindi il concetto filosofico del"l'unione tra l'uomo e il cielo". L'architettura e la tecnologia degli edifici più importanti del Tempio fra cui il Padiglione della Preghiera per il Buon Raccolto, l'Altare Circolare elevato e la Volta Celeste imperiale sono opere eminenti nella storia dell'architettonica cinese e costituiscono un importante e prezioso patrimonio artistico per il mondo intero.

I 24 imperatori delle dinastie Ming e Qing vi effettuarono ben 600 cerimonie di preghiera al Cielo. Il Tempio del Cielo costituisce un modello di perfezione dell'architettura cinese, ed al contempo, un ottimo referente di studio della politica, dell'astronomia, della conoscenza del calendario lunare, della filosofia, della musica, dei riti e della pittura dell'antica Cina.

Il Tempio del Cielo comprende una vasta superficie. Gli alti e robusti alberi presenti in gran numero all'interno del parco, circondano combinandosi armoniosamente con essi, gli eleganti elementi architettonici del Tempio, creando un ambiente dal carattere di una semplicità essenziale e solenne.

Patrimonio Mundial Cultural de Beijing: Templo del Cielo（西文）

Situado en el sureste de la zona urbana de Beijing, el Templo del Cielo se dedicaba en las dinastías Ming y Qing a las ceremonias imperiales de veneración al dios del cielo y a rogar por las buenas cosechas. La distribución y forma de su arquitectura reflejan la tradicional cosmología china del "Cielo esférico y tierra cuadrada" y "Armonía entre la Naturaleza y el ser humano". Las construcciones principales, como el Pabellón de las Rogativas por las Buenas Cosechas, el Altar de la Terraza Circular y la Bóveda Imperial del Cielo, representan el increíble nivel técnico y artístico y constituyen obras maestras y preciosos patrimonios en la historia arquitectónica de China y el mundo.

Además de su extraordinario arte constructivo, como sede de más de 600 ceremonias reverenciales, presididas por 22 emperadores, el inmueble tiene un alto valor para los estudios de aspectos como la política, astronomía, calendario, filosofía, música, ritos y pintura de la antigua China.

Sobre una superficie muy extendida del Templo del Cielo, el bosque de los viejos árboles y las arquitecturas rituales conforman una atmósfera rica en serenidad y solemnidad, que generan una especial atracción.

北京的世界文化遗产——明十三陵

位于北京北郊昌平区的明十三陵，是明朝迁都北京之后13位皇帝的陵墓群。整个陵区三面环山，唯有南面接北京平原，中间是约40平方千米的小盆地。十三座陵墓分布在东北西三面，各陵分别以一座山峰为背衬，可谓风水宝地、匠心独运。

十三座陵墓分别为明成祖长陵、仁宗献陵、宣宗景陵、英宗裕陵、宪法宗茂陵、孝宗泰陵、武宗康陵、世宗永陵、穆宗昭陵、神宗定陵、光宗庆陵、熹宗德陵、思宗思陵。陵墓规模大小不一，形制基本相同。

定陵是唯一开挖地宫并开放的陵墓，曾出土大量极为精美的文物。

World Cultural Heritage Sites in Beijing:
The Ming Tombs （英文）

The Ming Tombs are located in Changping District in northern Beijing. Here are buried 13 emperors of the Ming Dynasty. The entire mausoleum area is embraced by mountains in three directions, and its south section is separated from the Beijing Plain by a 40-square-kilometer basin. There are 13 tombs scattered in the north, east and west of the mausoleum area. Each tomb lies against a hill, in accordance with the traditional Chinese philosophy of *fengshui*.

The 13 tombs, named Changling, Xianling, Jingling, Yuling, Maoling, Tailing, Kangling, Yongling, Zhaoling, Dingling, Qingling, Deling and Siling, respectively, are similar in size and layout.

The Dingling Tomb is the only one that has been excavated, and is open to visitors. Many cultural relics have been unearthed from its underground palace.

北京の世界文化遺産－明の十三陵 （日文）

北京市北郊外の昌平区にある明の十三陵は、明が都を北京に遷した後の13人皇帝の陵墓群である。陵墓区は、三面は山々に取り囲まれ、南の一面だけは北京平原に連なり、中央は40k㎡の小さな盆地になって

いる。13の墓はそれぞれ東北西三面の山々に散在し、1つの墓はそれぞれ1つの峰を背にしている。いわば地相がすばらしい「風水宝地」である。

13の墓はそれぞれ成祖の長陵、仁宗の献陵、宣宗の景陵、英宗の裕陵、憲宗の茂陵、孝宗の泰陵、武宗の康陵、世宗の永陵、穆宗の昭陵、神宗の定陵、光宗の慶陵、熹宗の徳陵、思宗の思陵である。規模は大小さまざまだが、規格はほぼ同じである。

定陵は、地宮（墓室）が発掘を経て一般に開放されている唯一の墓で、かつてはおびただしい量の珍しい文物を出土した。

Weltkulturerbe Beijings:
Die Ming-Gräber （德文）

In der Umgebung Beijings gibt es drei Gräbergruppen der kaiserlichen Familien der beiden letzten Dynastien, nähmlich der Ming- und der Qing-Dynastie. Eine Gräbergruppe stellen die 13 Gräber der Kaiser und ihrer Frauen bzw. ihrer Konkubinen der Ming-Dynastie dar. Die anderen zwei Gräbergruppen sind Gräber der neun Kaiser und ihrer Familien der Qing-Dynastie.

Die Ming-Gräber liegen in einem 40 Quadratkilometer großen Becken am Fuß des Tianshou-Berges innerhalb des Bezirkes Chanping im Nordwesten Beijings. 13 der 16 Kaiser der Ming-Dynastie fanden hier zusammen mit ihren Familien ihre letzte Ruhestätte. Zu diesen 13 Kaisergräbern gehören das Grab Changling für den Kaiser Cheng Zu, das Grab Xinling für den Kaiser Ren Zong, das Grab Jingling für den

Kaiser Xuan Zong, das Grab Yuling für den Kaiser Ying Zong, das Grab Maoling für den Kaiser Xuan Zong, das Grab Tailing für den Kaiser Xiao Zong), das Grab Kangling für den Kaiser Wu Zong, das Grab Yongling für den Kaiser Shi Zong, das Grab Zhaoling für den Kaiser Mu Zong, das Grab Dingling für den Kaiser Shen Zong), das Grab Qingling für den Kaiser Guang Zong) , das Grab Deling für den Kaiser Xi Zong und das Grab Siling für den Kaiser Si Zong.

Das Grab Dingling wurde im Jahre 1956 geöffnet. Bei Freillegung wurden zahlreiche kostbare Grabbeigeben gefunden. Es ist das einzige freigelegte und für Besucher bestimmte Grab von den 13 Ming-Gräbern.

Sites du patrimoine mondial à Beijing
Les Treize Tombeaux des Ming （法文）

Situés dans l'arrondissement de Changping aux environs nord de Beijing, les Treize Tombeaux des Ming sont la nécropole de 13 empereurs qui gouvernèrent l'Etat après le transfert de leur capitale à Beijing. Entourée de montagnes sur trois côtés et donnant sur la plaine de Beijing au sud, la nécropole occupe un petit bassin d'environ 40 kilomètres carrés. Ces 13 tombeaux se disséminent aux lisières est, nord et ouest du petit bassin et chacun est adossé à une montagne. On peut dire que cette situation géographique serait très favorable du point de vue de la géomancie.

Les Treize Tombeaux des Ming sont respectivement le Changling de l'empereur Chengzu, le Xianling de l'empereur Renzong, le Jingling de l'empereur Xuanzong, le Yuling de l'empereur Yingzong, le Maoling de l'empereur Xianzong, le Tailing de l'empereur Xiaozong, le Kangling de l'empereur Wuzong, le Yongling de l'empereur Shizong, le Zhaoling de l'empereur Muzong, le Dingling de l'empereur Shenzong, le Qingling de l'empereur Guangzong, le Deling de l'empereur Xizong et le Siling de l'empereur Sizong. Malgré leurs tailles variées, leurs formes et les systèmes funéraires observés lors de leur construction étaient essentiellement pareils.

Le Dingling est la seule tombe à être exhumée et ouverte au tourisme avec son palais souterrain de laquelle ont été déterrées un grand nombre de pièces d'une finesse extrême.

① 十三陵长陵鸟瞰
A bird's-eye view of the Changling Tomb
十三陵の長陵ちょかん
조감한 십삼능 장능
Panorama du Changling des Treize Tombeaux des Ming
Panorama der 13 Ming-Gräber
Una vista dall'alto della tomba Changling delle 13 Tombe dei Ming
Чанлин с птичьего вида
Vista panorámica del mausoleo Changling de las Trece Tumbas

베이징의 세계문화유산 - 명십삼능 (韓文)

베이징 북쪽교외 창핑구(昌平區)에 위치해 있는 명십삼능(明十三陵)은 명나라가 베이징에 천도한 다음 집정한 13명 황제의 능묘이다. 삼면이 산에 둘러 쌓이고 남쪽에만 베이징 평원을 마주하고 있는데 중간은 약 40㎢의 작은 분지가 있다. 명십삼능은 동쪽, 북쪽, 서쪽에 분포되어 있으며 각 능마다 하나의 산봉우리를 등지고 있는데 명당자리로 만들기 위해 공력을 넣은 것을 알아볼 수 있다.

13 개의 능묘로는 명성조의 장능(長陵), 인종의 헌능(獻陵), 현종의 경능(景陵), 영종의 유능(裕陵), 헌법종의 무능(茂陵), 효종의 태능(泰陵), 무종의 강능(康陵), 세종의 영능(永陵), 목종의 소능(昭陵), 신종의 정능(定陵), 광종의 경능(慶陵), 희종의 덕능(德陵), 사종의 사능(思陵) 등이 있는데 규모가 서로 다르지만 형태는 기본상 비슷하다.

현재 정능만이 유일하게 발굴하고 개방한 능묘인데 여기서 대량의 아주 정교한 문물들이 출토 되었다.

Patrimonio Cultural de la Humanidad de Beijing: Trece Tumbas de la Dinastía Ming (西文)

Las Trece Tumbas de la Dinastía Ming se sitúan en el suburbio norteño de la ciudad, donde yacen los restos de 13 emperadores posteriores al traslado de la capital de Nanjing a Beijing, realizado durante ese mandato. Extendida en una cuenca de 40 Km² de superficie, la zona de los mausoleos está rodeada por tres de sus lados por la montaña y por el sur aparece la planicie. Según la teoría de Feng-shui, las trece tumbas están en el Oeste, Este y Norte y cada una se apoya en una colina como respaldo.

Las tumbas, de similar forma, pero diferentes tamaños, son los mausoleos Changling, del emperador Chengzu, Xianling, del emperador Renzong, Jingling, del emperador Xuanzong, Yuling, del emperador Yingzong, Maoling, del emperador Xianzong, Tailing, del emperador Xiaozong, Kangling, del emperador Wuzong, Yongling, del emperador Shi, Zhaoling, del emperador Muzong, Dingling, del emperador Shenzong, Qingling, del emperador Guangzong, Deling, del emperador Xizong, y Siling, del emperador Sizong. De ellos, el único explorado y abierto al público es el de Ding, donde desenterraron gran cantidad de exquisitos objetos.

① 十三陵永陵
The Yongling Tomb
十三陵の永陵
십삼능 영능
Le Yongling des Treize Tombeaux des Ming
Das Yongling-Grab
La tomba Yongling delle 13 Tombe dei Ming
Юнлин из могил Шисаньлина
Mausoleo Yongling de las Trece Tumbas

Le tredici Tombe dei Ming, patrimonio culturale mondiale a Pechino（意大利文）

Situate nel distretto di Changping nella periferia settentrionale di Pechino, le tredici Tombe dei Ming sono un gruppo di mausolei dei 13 imperatori della dinastia Ming che regnarono a Pechino dopo il trasferimento della capitale da Nanchino. La parte orientale, occidentale e settentrionale dell'area di tombe è circondata da monti mentre la parte meridionale è segnata dalla pianura di Pechino. Al centro vi si trova un bacino di ben 40 chilometri quadrati di superaficie.

Le 13 tombe sono situate rispettivamente a est, nord e ovest, e si chiamano: il mausoleo Changling dell'imperatore Chengzu, il mausoleo Xianling dell'imperatore Renzong, il mausoleo Jingling dell'imperatore Xuanzong, il mausoleo Yuling dell'imperatore Yingzong, il mausoleo Maoling dell'imperatore Xianzong, il mausoleo Tailing dell'imperatore Xiaozong, il mausoleo Kangling dell'imperatore Wuzong, il mausoleo Yongling dell'imperatore Shizong, il mausoleo Zhaoling dell'imperatore Muzong, il mausoleo Dingling dell'imperatore Shenzong, il mausoleo Qingling dell'imperatore Guangzong, il mausoleo Deling dell'imperatore Xizong e il mausoleo Siling dell'imperatore Sizong. La dimensione delle tombe varia ma la struttra segue lo stesso schema standardizzato.

Мировое культурное наследие – Шисаньлин (могилы минских императоров)（俄文）

Могилы императоров династии Мин (Шисаньлин) находятся в районе Чанпине города Пекина. Здесь покоятся 13 минских императоров. Этот мемориальный комплекс окружен горами о трех сторон. На юге впадины, площадью 40 кв.км. соединен с пекинской равниной. Могилы расположены на востоке, севере и западе. Гора служит фоном каждой могилы.

Могилы императоров династии Мин – это Чанлин, Сянлин, Цзинлин, Юйлин, Маолин, Тайлин, Канлин, Юнлин, Чжаолин, Динлин, Цинлин, Дэлин и Сылин. Масштаб каждой могилы разен, но форма в основном одинакова.

Динлин – единая раскопанная гробница и открытая для публики. Здесь были обнаружены многие исторические древности.

② 武臣
Military Officers
Généraux
Generale
Ufficiale di armata
Oficial de la armada.
무신
武臣
Военноначальник

③ 勋臣
Ministers of Merit
Ministre de mérites
Verdienster Minister
Ministro onoraio
Ministro honorífico.
훈신
勛臣
Заслуженный министр

④ 麒麟
Stone Qilin
Licorne
Fabeltier Qilin
Statua di Qilin
Estatua de un *qinlin*.
기린
麒麟
Каменный Цилин

⑤⑥ 定陵地宫
Underground Palace
定陵の地下宮殿(墓室)
정릉의 지하궁전
Tomba ipogeica nel Dingling
Der unterirdische Palast des Dingling-Grabes
Le palais souterrain du Dingling
Palacio Subterráneo de la Tumba Dingling
Подземный дворец Динлина

⑦ 定陵明楼
The Soul Tower
定陵の明楼
정릉의 명루
La Tour de la stèle du Dingling
Der Pavillon dar Klarheit des
Dingling-grabes
La Torre delle steli di Dingling
Torre de los Espiritus de Dingling
Минлоу

北京的世界文化遗产——周口店

　　周口店北京猿人遗址位于北京西南房山区周口店龙骨山脚下。1929 年 12 月，中国考古学家古人类学家裴文中先生在龙骨山发掘出第一颗完整的"北京人"头盖骨化石。"北京人"已学会使用原始的工具，懂得使用火和保存火种。"北京人"距今约五六十万年，它的发现奠定了直立人在人类发展中的地位，为人类起源提供了大量的、富有说明力的证据。

World Cultural Heritage Sites in Beijing:
The Peking Man Site at Zhoukoudian （英文）

The Peking Man Site lies at the foot of Longgu Hill near Zhoukoudian Village, in southwestern Beijing's Fangshan District. In December 1929, a Chinese paleoanthropologist named Pei Wenzhong discovered a complete skull of "Peking Man" on Longgu Hill. Archeological findings indicate that Peking Man could use simple tools and fire, and preserve kindling. The discovery of Peking Man, who dates back nearly 600,000 years, illustrates the evolution of homo erectus and provides abundant evidences of the origin of the human species.

北京の世界文化遺産－周口店北京原人遺跡 （日文）

　　周口店北京原人遺跡は北京市西南房山区周口店竜骨山麓にある。1929 年 12 月、中国の考古学者で古人類学者の裴文中先生は竜骨山ではじめて最初の完全な「北京人」の頭蓋骨化石を発見した。「北京人」はすでに原始道具の開発に成功し、火の使用と火種の保管を知っていた。「北京人」は今から約 50－60 万年前の原人で、その頭蓋骨の発見は人類発展の過程における直立人間の地位が確立され、人類起源を研究するために大量な説得力のある証拠を提供している。

베이징의 세계문화 유산 – 저우커우덴 북경원인 유적 （韩文）

　　저우커우덴북경원인유적은 베이징 서남쪽 팡산구(房山區) 저우커우덴 룽구산(龍骨山) 기슭에 있다. 1929 년 12 월 중국의 고고학자이며 고인류학자인 페이원중(裴文中)은 룽구산에서 최초로 완전한 "북경원인"의 두개골 화석을 발굴해 냈다. 당시의 "북경원인"는 이미 원시적인 도구를 사용할줄 알며 불을 사용하는 것과 불을 보존하는 방법을 알고 있었다. "북경원인"은 지금으로부터 5, 6 천년전에 생존했으며 이 발견은 인류발전 중의 직립보행의 위치를 결정하였으며 인류기원의 연구에 대량적인. 설명가치가 있는 증거를 제공하였다.

Sites du patrimoine mondial à Beijing: Le site de l'Homme de Beijing （法文）

Le site de l'Homme de Beijing est situé au pied de la colline Longgu (os de dragon) dans l'arrondissement de Fangshan aux environs sud-ouest de Beijing. En 1929, Monsieur Pei Wenzhong, archéologue et paléontologiste chinois, découvrit la première calotte crânienne intacte de l'Homme de Beijing. Ce dernier savait déjà se servir des instruments primitifs, exploiter et conserver le feu. L'Homme de Beijing aurait vécu 500 000 ans avant nous. Sa découverte a affirmé la place de l'*Homo erectus* dans l'évolution de l'Homme, fournissant quantité de preuves persuasives.

Patrimonio Cultural de la Humanidad de Beijing:
Sitio del Hombre de Pekín, en Zhoukoudian （西文）

Al pie de la montaña Longgushan (Hueso de Dragón), en el distrito Fangshan, al suroeste de Beijing, en diciembre de 1929, Pei Wenzhong, arqueólogo y paleo-antropólogo chino, encontró el fósil del primer cráneo completo del Hombre de Pekín, que data de 500.000 a 600.000 años atrás, y ya dominaba el uso de algunas herramientas primordiales, además de utilizar y preservar el fuego. Este descubrimiento determinó la posición de los erectos en la evolución del ser humano y brindó gran cantidad de pruebas sobre el origen de nuestra especie.

Il sito dell'Uomo di Pechino di Zhoukoudian, patrimonio culturale mondiale a Pechino （意大利文）

Situato ai piedi del monte Longgushan (monte dell'Osso del Drago) a Zhoukoudian nel distretto di Fangshan, a sud-ovest di Pechino. Nel dicembre del 1929, l'antropologo cinese Pei Wenzhong e il suo gruppo di archeologi vi scoprirono il cranio di un uomo vissuto in questa regione circa mezzo milione di anni fa. A quell'epoca l'Uomo di Pechino faceva uso di utensili in osso e in pietra e sapeva fare uso del fuoco e mantenerlo acceso. La sua scoperta premise di stabilire la posizione dell'Uomo Sapiens nel corso dello sviluppo umano e fornì un importante esemplare per la ricerca sull'origine degli esseri umani.

Мировое культурное наследие – первобытная стоянка «Пекинского синантропа» Чжоукоудянь （俄文）

　　Стоянка пекинского синантропа Чжоукоудянь находится на горе Лунгушань, в 50 км к юго-западу от города Пекина. В декабре 1929 г. китайский археолог Пэй Вэнчжун обнаружил в лунгушаньской пещере первый целый череп пекинского синанстропа. Пекинский синантроп умеет пользоваться первобытными инструментами, огнем и хранить огонь. 500 – 600 тыс. лет назад пекинский синантроп жил в пещерах горы Лунгушань. Его обнаружение предоставляет много сильных доказательств для изучения источника человека.

Weltkulturerbe Beijings: Die Heimstätte des Peking-Menschen in Zhoukoudian （德文）

Sie liegt in einer Höhle am Fuß des Longgu-Berges in Zhoukoudian des Bezirkes Fangshan im Südwesten Beijings. Im Dezember 1929 entdeckte hier der Paläoanthropologe Pei Wenzhong die erste vollständig erhaltende Schädeldecke des Peking-Menschen (*Sinanthropus pekinensis*). Später wurden hier noch einige Affenmenschenfossilien, beigelegte Gegenstände, Fossilen von Tieren ausgebraben. Experten meinen, dass der Peking-Mensch vor 500 000 bis 600 000 Jahren leben begann. Er wohnte in Höhlen unb betrieb Jagd, konnte schon Gegenstände aus Knochen herstellen und benutzten und verstand es, mit Feuer umzugehen. Die Funde sind für das Studium der Herkunft der Menschheit von großer Bedeutung.

北京的皇家园林——北海公园

北海公园在辽代就建有行宫，金代这里是金中都东北郊的行宫，并已有燕京八景"琼岛春荫"的名声。元大都更是以琼华岛为中心设计修建，北海变成皇城内的宫苑。明清紫禁城东移，北海称为西苑。

北海是保存最完整的皇家园囿，也是中国古典园林中的杰作。它是辽、金、元、明、清五个王朝的皇家宫苑，历时近900年，这在世界皇家园林中也是罕见的。

Imperial Gardens in Beijing: Beihai Park（英文）

As early as in the Liao Dynasty, a temporary imperial palace was built in today's Beihai Park, and then the Jin Dynasty built its temporary imperial palace here. The park is famous for the "Jade Islet in Spring," which is one of the Eight Scenes of Yanjing (Beijing). The Yuan Dynasty made Jade Islet the center of its capital, Dadu, and the park became an imperial garden. During the Ming and Qing dynasties, the imperial palace was moved eastward, and Beihai Park was then called West Garden.

As China's best-preserved imperial garden, Beihai Park is a masterpiece among classical Chinese gardens. Over 900 years, it consecutively served as an imperial garden of the Liao, Jin, Yuan, Ming and Qing Dynasties.

北京の世界文化遺産－北海（日文）

北海公園は、最初は遼代の行宮であったところで、金代に金の中都東北郊外の行宮となってからは「瓊島春蔭」の名で「燕京八景」の1つとして登場した。北京が元の大都となったときは、さらに瓊華島を中心として造園し皇室の庭園となった。明・清時代は、紫禁城が東に移ったため、北海はこれに対して西苑と名が改められた。

北海は最も完全な形に保たれた皇室庭園であり、中国の古典庭園の傑作である。900年にわたって遼、金、元、明、清5王朝の皇室庭園としての歴史は中断されたことなく、これも世界の皇室庭園の中にはまれに見るものである。

Sites du patrimoine mondial à Beijing: Le parc Beihai（法文）

Sous la dynastie des Liao, on édifia déjà un palais de plaisance sur l'emplacement du Parc Beihai et sous les Jin, l'emplacement était occupé par une résidence impériale secondaire dans la banlieue nord-est de Zhongdu, endroit connu sous l'appellation d'"Ombrages printaniers de l'île Qionghua", un des Huit Spectacles captivants de Yanjing. Sous les Yuan, l'île Qionghua devint le centre de Dadu, capitale de cette dynastie, et Beihai servait de jardin dans la Cité interdite. Sous les Ming et les Qing, la Cité interdite se déplaça vers l'est et Beihai était alors appelé "Jardin de l'Ouest". Pendant 900 ans, Beihait servait de parc impérial, ce qui est rarement vu parmi les parcs impériaux du monde.

Gartenanlge: Der Beihai-Park（德文）

Der Beihai-Park, auch der Nordsee-Park genannt, liegt im Nordwesten des Kaiserpalastes. Er ist mit der Entwicklung der Stadt Beijing eng verbunden. Schon während der Zeit der Liao- und Jin-Dynastie diente er als eine kaiserliche Residenz. In der Yuan-Dynastie wurde rings um den Nordsee die Hauptstadt Dadu erbaut. Zu jener Zeit gehörte der Beihai-Park zu einer wichtigen Gartenanlage innderhalb der Kaiserstadt. Während der Zeit der Ming- und der Qing-Dynastie wurde der Beihai-Park in großem Maßstab ausgebaut. Der Grundriß des Parkes, wie er während der Regierungsperiode des Qing-Kaisers Qian Long angelegt worden war, ist im großen und ganzen bis heute erhalten geblieben.

Parques Imperiales de Beijing: Palacio de Invierno（西文）

En las dinastías Liao y Jin, el Palacio de Invierno era el hospedaje provisional de los emperadores en su estancia fuera de la Ciudad Prohibida. Figuró entre los ocho paisajes más pintorescos de la capital, debido a la hermosura de su paisaje durante la primavera. En la dinastía Yuan, el lugar constituía el centro de todo el Palacio Imperial y se convirtió en Palacio Occidental, por el traslado del centro hacia el Este de la Ciudad Prohibida.

Como palacio mejor conservado, el lugar experimentó varios cambios en el transcurso de las dinastías Liao, Jin, Yuan, Ming y Qing y suma una historia de casi 900 años, algo muy poco visto entre otros palacios del mundo.

Il parco Beihai, giardino imperiale a Pechino （意大利文）

Il parco Beihai fu una residenza imperiale situata nella periferia nord-orientale della capitale della dinastia Jin, Zhongdu. Utilizzando l'edificio situato nell'isola Qionghua (Isola del Fiore di Giada) la dinastia Yuan ne fece il centro della propria capitale, Dadu, rendendo il parco Beihai il giardino imperiale all'interno della città imperiale. A seguito dello spostamento della Città Proibita verso est durante le successive dinastie Ming e Qing, il parco Beihai divenne il Giardino Occidentale. Anch'esso è uno splendido esempio di giardino imperiale ancora che oggi si conserva in ottimo stato. La sua storia di giardino imperiale comprende un ciclo durato ben 900 anni con una successione di dinastie che va dalla Liao, Jin e Yuan fino a quelle Ming e Qing.

Мировое культурное наследие—парк Бэйхай （俄文）

Парк был резиденцией династии Ляо, Цзинь, Юань, Мин и Цин. История парка насчитывается около 900 лет. Это редко встречается среди других императорских садов в мире. Взяв остров Цюнхуадао парка Бэйхай как центр, проектировали и построили юаньскую столицу. Тогда Бэйхай стал придворным садом в императорском городе. В династиях Мин и Цин Запретный город был перемещен на восток, в то время Бэйхай назывался Сыюань.

Парк Бэйхай – наиболее хорошо и целостно сохранившийся императорский сад, шедевр китайской классической садовой архитектуры.

베이징의 세계문화 유적 – 베이하이(北海) （韩文）

베이하이공원은 요나라시기에 이미 행궁이 건설되었다. 금나라시기에 베하이공원은 금나라 중도(中都) 동북 교외의 행궁이였으며 연경팔경(燕京八景) 중의 "경도춘음(璚島春蔭)"이라는 명성을 가지고 있었다. 원나라 대도는 더욱 충다오섬을 중심으로 증축하였는데 베이하이를 황궁의 정원으로 탈바꿈 시켰다. 명·청나라시기에는 쯔진청을 동쪽으로 옮기면서 베이하이를 서원이라고 불렀다.

베이하이는 지금까지 가장 완전하게 보존된 황가 정원으로 중국고전조경의 걸작이기도 하다. 베이하이는 요, 금, 원, 명, 청 다섯개 왕조의 황궁 정원으로서 900 년동안의 역사를 가지고 있으며 세계황가원림 중에서 아주 희소한 것이다.

北海阅古楼三希堂法帖石刻
Stone inscriptions by renowned ancient calligrapher, housed on the Jade Islet.
北海閣古楼の三希堂法帖石刻
베하이 열고루 삼희당법첩 석각
Calligraphies sculptées sur pierre conservées dans la Salle des Trois Modèles d'écriture (Sanxitang) du pavillon Yuegu dans le parc Beihai.
Steinschitzerei von der Sanxitang-Kalligrafievorlage, im Yuegu-Turm des Beihai-Parkes aufbewahrt
Una raccolta di tavole recanti le iscrizioni di famosi calligrafi e poeti cinesi conservata nel Padiglione per la Lettura dei Classici (Yuegulou) nel Parco Beihai.
Камни с высеченными надписями «Саньситан Фате» в павильоне Юегулоу парка Бэйхай
En el Edificio Yuegu del Palacio del Invierno se conserva la inscripción lapidaria de tres excelentes obras de caligrafía que el emperador Qianlong coleccionaba.

北京的皇家园林——景山

　　景山位于北京城的中轴线上，在紫禁城正北，为皇家御苑，景山有五个山峰，上面各建有一个亭子，中间万春亭为老北京登高眺望故宫及京城全景的最好去处。

　　景山东坡上，原有一棵老槐树，1644年，李自成农民起义军攻进北京，明代末皇帝崇祯逃到这里自杀。

Imperial Gardens in Beijing: Jingshan Park（英文）

Formerly an imperial garden, Jingshan Park lies to the north of the Forbidden City on the north-south axis of Beijing. Prospect Hill in the park has five peaks, on each of which stands a pavilion. The Pavilion of Everlasting Spring in the middle is an ideal place from which to view the Forbidden City and the panorama of Beijing.

There was an old Chinese scholar tree on the east slope of Prospect Hill. In 1644, when Li Zicheng led his rebel troops to take Beijing, Emperor Chongzhen of the Ming Dynasty hung himself on the tree.

景山公園（日文）

北京の南北を貫く中軸線上、紫禁城の真北にある。皇室庭園にあたるところであって、5つの峰の上にはそれぞれ1つのこじんまりしたあずまやがある。真ん中のは万春亭と呼ばれるもので、故宮ひいては北京市街全体を眺める最適な場所である。

景山東の山腹に、かつて1本のえんじゅの木があった。1644年、李自成が率いる農民蜂起軍が北京に攻め込んだとき、明のラストエンペラーの崇禎帝がここに逃げてきて、首つりして自ら絶った。

징산(景山)공원（韓文）

징산은 베이징성의 중축선에 있고 쯔진청의 정북방향에 있는 황가어원이며 징산에는 다섯 봉우리가 있고 봉마다 정자를 세웠는데 가운데의 완춘팅(萬春亭)은 베이징에서 고궁과 베이징성을 한눈에 내려다 볼 수 있는 좋은 곳 이다.

징산의 동쪽에 괴목이 한 그루 있었는데 1644년 이자성(李自成)농민군이 베이징을 함락할 때 명나라 말대 황제 숭정제(崇禎帝)가 이 나무에 목을 매고 자살 했다고 한다.

Il parco Jingshan (Parco della Collina della Contemplazione)（意大利文）

Si trova di fronte alla Shenwumen (Porta settentrionale del Palazzo imperiale) lungo l'asse centrale su cui la città di Pechino è stata edificata: il parco Jingshan era il parco imperiale. Di fronte alla sua entrata meridionale si erge una bella torre di osservazione, mentre un viottolo si snoda sulla collina centrale, portando al Wanchunting (padiglione dell'Eterna Primavera), il più grande dei cinque padiglioni costruite su cinque colline. Da qui si gode di una stupenda vista sul centro di Pechino, e sulla Città Proibita.

Lungo il pendio orientale è presente un'antica conifera della specie conosciuta in cinese come "albero del letterato" in cui nel 1644 l'ultimo imperatore Ming si tolse la vita quando le truppe ribelli di contadini dirette da Li Zicheng attaccarono Pechino.

Парк Цзиншань（俄文）

Находится на оси Пекина, на севере от Запретного города. Является императорским садом. На каждом из 5 пиков горы Цзиншань была построена беседка. С беседки Ваньчунтин можно полюбоваться всем великолепием архитектурного комплекса Гугуна и всем городом.

На восточном склоне горы Цзиншань была софора. В 1644 г. вождь восставших Ли Цзычэн взял Пекин, последний минский император Чунчжэнь повесился именно у этой софоры.

Parque de la Colina Jingshan（西文）

La Colina Jingshan se ubica al norte de la Ciudad Prohibida, también en el eje central de Beijing. Como jardín imperial, cuenta con 5 picos y por encima de cada uno se yergue un quiosco. El Wanchun, sobre el pico central, era lugar ideal para captar una vista panorámica del recinto imperial y la antigua capital.

La Colina Jingshan se ubica al norte de la Ciudad Prohibida, también en el eje central de Beijing. Como jardín imperial, cuenta con 5 picos y por encima de cada uno se yergue un quiosco. El Wanchun, sobre el pico central, era lugar ideal para captar una vista panorámica del recinto imperial y la antigua capital.

En 1644, al enterarse de la entrada en Beijing de un ejército de campesinos rebeldes dirigido por su líder, Li Zicheng, el último emperador del periodo Ming, Chongzhen, escapó de la Ciudad Prohibida, pero más tarde, presa de la desesperación, se suicidó colgándose de un árbol de sófora china en la cuesta oriental de la colina.

Le Parc Jingshan（法文）

Située sur l'axe central de la ville de Beijing au nord de la Cité interdite, la Colline aux beaux paysages (Jingshan) était un jardin impérial. Elle comprend cinq sommets surmontés chacun d'un kiosque. Le kiosque central du Printemps éternel (Wanchunting) était le meilleur endroit pour avoir une vue panoramique sur le Palais impérial et sur toute la ville de Beijing.

Sur le versant est de la Colline Jingshan poussait à l'origine un vieux sophora auquel Chongzhen, dernier empereur de la dynastie des Ming, se pendit en 1644 lorsque les troupes rebelles de Li Zicheng assaillaient Beijing.

Der Jingshan-Park（德文）

Der Jingshan-Park liegt im Norden des Kaiserpalastes. In der Zeit der Ming- und Qing-Dynastie war er eine kaiserliche Parkanlage. Der Hauptteil des Parkes ist der Jingshan-Berg, auch den Kohlen-Berg genannt. Der Berg hat fünf Gipfel, auf denen während der Regierungsperiode des Qing-Kaisers Qianlong fünf Pavillons gebaut wurden. Der Wanshou-Pavillon auf der mittleren Gipfel war der höchste Punkt der Innenstadt Beijings.

Am östlichen Berghang wuchs früher ein alter Akazienbaum. Im Jahre 1644, als sich das ausständige Bauernheer unter Führung Li Zichengs Beijing näherte, hatte sich der letzte Ming-Kaiser Chong Zhen hier an diesem Baum erhängt.

北京的皇家园林——香山

香山是北京西郊自然风景园林。这里夏季清凉，一度成为皇帝避暑行宫。清乾隆年间扩建改名为静宜园，与静明园的玉泉山、清漪园的万寿山并称"三山"，可惜被英法联军和八国联军焚毁。使香山驰名的是遍岭的黄栌，一到霜秋，便是"霜叶红于二月花"。

Imperial Gardens in Beijing: Fragrant Hills Park（英文）

Fragrant Hills Park, in the western suburbs of Beijing, is famous for its natural scenery. The climate is pleasant in summer, so some emperors built temporary summer palaces here. Emperor Qianlong of the Qing Dynasty renamed it Jingyi Garden. The Fragrant Hills, the Jade Spring Hill in the Jingming Garden and the Longevity Hill in the Qingyi Garden are collectively called the "Three Hills." However, the Jingyi Garden was burned to the ground by the invading Anglo-French Allied Forces in 1860 and the Eight-Power Allied Forces in 1900. Maple trees dye the hillsides red in late autumn.

香山公園（日文）

香山公園は北京市西部郊外の自然景色がすばらしいところである。夏は涼しいため、一度は皇帝の避暑行宮となっていた。清の乾隆年間に増改築を経て静宜園と名が改められ、静明園の玉泉山、清漪園の万寿山とともに「三山」と併称されていた。残念ながら8カ国連合軍によって焼き払われてしまった。もみじは香山の名物である。毎年の秋になると、山一面は燃えるようなもみじに覆われ、これを見に観光客は殺到する。

Парк Сяншань（俄文）

Парк Сяншань находится в западном пригороде Пекина. Летом здесь прохладно. Парк был летней резиденцией императора. В годы правления цинского императора Цяньлун парк был расширен и переименован в Цзинъйюань. Он, гора Юйцюаньшань в саду Цзинминъюань и гора Ваньшоушань вместе называются Саньшань (три горы). Жаль, парк был сожжен англо-французскими войсками и войсками из 8 стран. теперь, когда осень наступает, везде на горе Сяньшань красные листья.

상산(香山)공원（韩文）

상산은 베이징 서쪽 교외의 자연풍경원림으로 여름에 서늘하여 한때는 황제의 피서행궁으로 사용되었다. 청나라 건륭년간에는 증축하여 정의원(靜宜園)이라고 개칭하였으며 상산과 정의원의 위취안산(玉泉山) 및 칭이위안의 완서우산을 합칭하여 "삼산(三山)"이라고 불렸다. 아쉬운 것은 영국, 프랑스 연합군과 팔국연합군에 의하여 파괴당했다. 상산을 유명하게 만든 된 것은 늦가을에 온 산을 물들이는 옷나무 단풍이다. 옷나무에 단풍이 들면 마치 노을처럼 붉게 타올라 상산을 현란하고 아름답게 장식한다.

Parque de la Colina Perfumada（西文）

Fue su paisaje natural lo que hizo famosa a la Colina Perfumada, en el suburbio occidental de Beijing. Debido a su frescura y temperatura adecuada en el verano, al principio se levantaron allí los palacios destinados al veraneo de los emperadores. Durante el reinado del emperador Qianlong, de la dinastía Qing, se ordenó ampliar las construcciones y bautizarlas como Parque Jingyi, que en aquel entonces conformaron las "Tres Colinas", junto a la Yuquan del Parque Jingming y la Wanshou del Parque Qingyi, incendiadas en una oportunidad por los invasores anglo-franceses, que repitieron años más tarde el saqueo y la destrucción junto a otras seis potencias. Hoy, una espectacular vista de la colina son las rojas hojas de fustete, cuyo intenso color cubre completamente las elevaciones cuando llega el otoño.

Il parco delle Colline Profumate（意文）

Situato nella periferia occidentale di Pechino, il parco della Colline Profumate è caratterizzato da un paesaggio naturale. Grazie al fresco durante la stagione estiva, esso fu residenza imperiale per sfuggire dal caldo torrido e umido della lunga estate pechinese. Durante il periodo del regno dell'imperatore Qianlong della dinastia Qing, dopo essere stato ampliato il parco fu chiamato Giardino della Bellezza Limpida. Insieme alla Collina della Sorgente di Giada nel Giardino Jingming e la collina della Longevità nel Giardino Qingyi, fu denominato anche *Sanshan* (Tre colline). Al pari di tanti altri complessi di Pechino, anche questo nel 1860 e nel 1900 venne devastato e, fatta eccezione per una pagoda, nulla riuscì a salvarsi dalle fiamme. La stagione migliore per una visita è il tardo autunno, quando gli alberi si ricoprono di fogliame rosso fiammante, da sempre cantate dai poeti: in primavera e all'inizio dell'autunno le piante hanno invece fiori rosati simili a piume che viste in lontananza hanno la parvenza di nebbia illuminata dal sole.

Le Parc de la Colline parfumée（法文）

La Colline parfumée (Xiangshan) est un parc aux paysages naturels dans la banlieue ouest de Beijing. En été, il y fait frais et de ce fait, elle servait de villégiature aux empereurs. Agrandi sous le règne Qianlong de l'empereur Gaozong des Qing, elle fut rebaptisée le "Jardin de la Tranquillité (Jingyiyuan) et était une des "Trois Collines" avec la Colline de la Fontaine de jade (Yuquanshan) du Jardin de la Pure Clarté (Jingmingyuan) et la Colline de la Longévité millénaire (Wanshoushan) du Jardin des Vagues claires (Qingyiyuan). Malheureusement, le Jardin de la Tranquillité fut incendié par l'Armée alliée anglo-française et les troupes coalisées des Huit Puissances. Ce sont les fustets communs qui, poussant par monts et par vaux, ont rendu la Colline parfumée renommée. En automne, elle est recouverte d'un manteau pourpre.

Der Xiangshan-Park（德文）

Der Xiangshan-Park liegt im Bezirk Haidian, 20 km vom Stadtzentrum Beijings entfernt. Von der Jin- bis zur Ming-Dynastie diente er als eine kaiserliche Residenz. Während der Regierungsperiode des Qing-Kaisers Qian Long wurde hier am Fuß des Xiangshan-Berges der Jingyi-Garten (Garten der Wohltuenden Stille) angelegt. Der Xiangshan-Berg, auch der Duftende Berg genannt, gehört heute zu den Westbergen Bejings. In der Qing-Zeit zählte er mit dem Yuquan-Berg im Jingming-Garten und dem Wanshou-Berg im Qingyi-Garten zu den drei berühmten Bergen. Im Herbst leuchten die Ahornmblätter an Berghängen in verschiedensten Rottönen. Ein Blick, an dem sich die stadtbewohner seit langem Jahr für Jahr erfreuen.

香山红叶
Autumn maple on the Fragrant Hills
香山もみじ
상산의 단풍
Forêt au feuillage pourpré sur les Collines parfumées
Herbstlandschaft des Xiangshan-Parkes
Il paesaggio delle Colline profumate coperte dalle foglie rosse
Красные листья на горе Сяншань
Hojas rojas de la Colina Perfumada

北京的皇家园林——圆明园

被称为"万园之园"和"东方凡尔赛宫"的圆明园始建于清康熙四十八年（1709年），占地约350万平方米，规模宏大，集中国古代园林艺术之大成，同时还有由郎世宁等西方传教士设计的部分西式园林建筑。

1860年英、法联军和1900年八国联军两次洗劫和烧毁，使圆明园遭到彻底毁灭，仅剩少量断垣残壁。

Imperial Gardens in Beijing: Yuanmingyuan （英文）

Called the King of Gardens and the Oriental Palace of Versailles, Yuanmingyuan (Garden of Perfect Brightness) was first built in 1709, the 48th year of the reign of Emperor Kangxi of the Qing Dynasty. Covering 350 hectares, the park demonstrates the highest gardening techniques of ancient China. Foreign missionaries, including Giuseppe Castiglione, participated in the design of some Western-style structures in the park.

In 1860, the park was plundered and ruined by the Anglo-French Allied Forces, and then the Eight-Power Allied Forces burned it to the ground in 1900, leaving only a few collapsed walls.

원명원 （韩文）

"만원지원(萬元之園)"과 "동방의 베르사유궁전"이라고 불리웠던 원명원은 청나라 강희 48년 (1709년)에 건축되었으며 면적이 약 350 만 ㎡에 달하고 규모가 방대하여 중국 고대원림예술의 큰 성과였다. 원명원에는 카스틸리오네 등 서방 전도사들이 설계한 서양식 원림 건축물이 있었다.

1860 년 영국, 프랑스 연합군과 1900 년 팔국연합국에 의해 두 번이나 약탈과 파괴를 당한 원명원은 완전히 파괴되었는데 지금은 흔적만 남았을 뿐이다.

円明園 （日文）

円明園は「万之園」と「東洋のベルサイユ」の称がある庭園で、築造は清の康熙四十八年（1709年）にはじまり、敷地は350万㎡、中国造園芸術の粋を集めた規模が大きい庭園である。カスティグ・ライオネら西洋宣教師が設計した西洋スタイルの建物がある。

1860年英仏連合軍と1900年の8カ国連合軍の2回にわたる破壊と略奪を経て、一部の断垣残壁をのぞけば、徹底的に壊滅されてしまった。

Le Jardin de la Perfection et de la Clarté （法文）

L'aménagement du Jardin de la Perfection et de la Clarté (Yuanmingyuan), connu pour être "Jardin aux dix mille jardins" et le "Château de Versailles d'Orient", remonte à l'An 48 du règne Kangxi (1709) de l'empereur Shengzu des Qing. Couvrant 3,5 kilomètres carrés, ce jardin non seulement intégra les éléments essentiels de l'art des jardins chinois, mais possédait aussi des édifices jardiniers de style occidental conçus par des missionnaires européens comme l'Italien Giuseppe Castiglione.

Saccagé et incendié en 1860 par l'Armée alliée anglo-française et en 1900 par les troupes coalisées des Huit Puissances, ce chef-d'œuvre de l'art des jardins chinois fut complètement détruit. Aujourd'hui, il ne reste que des ruines.

Ruine des Yuanming-Gartens （德文）

Die Ruine des Yuanming-Gartens liegt am nordwestlichen Stadtrand Beijings. Der Yuanming-Garten wurde im 48. Regierungsjahr (1709) des Qing-Kaisers Qian Long angelegt. Er nam eine Fläche von 3,5 Millionen Quadratmetern ein. Damals war er als „Garten der Gärten" und „Château de Versailles des Ostens" bekannt. Hier gab auch Parkanlagen, die von dem italienischen Missionar und Maler Giuseppe Castiglione und anderen europäischen Künstlern entworfen wurden.

Bedauerlicherweise wurde dieser prächtige Garten, der unzählige Kulturrelikte und Kostbarkeiten beherbergte, wurde im 1860 von der englisch-französischen Interventionsarmee und dann im Jahre 1900 von der alliriten Interventionsaemee der achte Mächte geplündert und niedergebrannt.

Lo *Yuanmingyuan* (Giardino dello Splendore Rilucente) （意大利文）

Chiamato anche "Giardino dentro il Giardino" o "Versailles d'Oriente" lo Yuanmingyuan fu costruito nel 1709 (48° anno del regno dell'imperatore Kangxi della dinastia Qing) su una superficie di 350 ettari. Al suo interno erano combinate insieme l'antica arte dei giardini classici cinesi e l'arte dei giardini occidentali, un'opera realizzata da alcuni missionari occidentali fra cui il più noto fu l'italiano Giuseppe Castiglione.

Le truppe anglo-francesi e le forze alleate di Otto potenze presenti a Pechino fra il 1860 e il 1900, distrussero l'intero complesso di cui ora rimangono soltanto i resti sparsi sul suolo.

Юаньминъюань （俄文）

Строительство парка Юаньминъюань, который еще называется «восточный Версаль», начиналось с 1709 г. Площадь парка – около 3,5 млн. кв. м. В масштабном Юаньминъюань были не только китайские классические сады, но и сады и сооружения западного стиля, проектированные Гиузеппе Кастильоне (китайское имя – Лан Шинин) и другими западными миссионерами.

В 1860 году солдаты англо-французской армии и в 1900 году войска из 8 стран разнесли данную великолепный парк по кирпичам.

Ruina de Yuanmingyuan （西文）

El jardín Yuanmingyuan, conocido como el "Jardín de jardines" y "Versalles del Oriente", se comenzó a construir en 1709, 48° año del reinado del emperador Kangxi, de la dinastía Qing. Sobre 3,5 millones de m², fueron maravillosamente distribuidas obras arquitectónicas de variados estilos de China y Occidente, que compitieron entre sí por su belleza. El pintor Giuseppe Castiglione y otros misioneros occidentales se encargaron de diseñar la segunda parte.

En 1860 las tropas anglo-francesas saquearon e incendiaron Yuanmingyuan, acción que ambas naciones repitieron en 1900, junto con los ejércitos de otras seis potencias aliadas, dejando el lugar en la ruina total. Hoy sólo unos tallados rotos de mármol blanco permanecen en pie.

文化古迹——卢沟桥

位于北京西南永定河上的卢沟桥，有"卢沟晓月"的盛名，而1937年7月7日的"卢沟桥事变"又是从这里点燃了抗日战争的烈火，使卢沟桥成为具有重大历史意义的纪念地。

卢沟桥全长266.5米，桥两侧有261根望柱。柱上布满雕刻的石狮485只，为石刻艺术精品。

Lugou (Marco Polo) Bridge （英文）

The Lugou Bridge spans the Yongding River in the southwestern suburbs of Beijing. The "Lugou Bridge in the Moonlight" is one of the Eight Scenes of Yanjing. The Lugou Bridge Incident, occurring on July 7, 1937, marked the beginning of the Chinese People's War of Resistance against Japanese Aggression, which made the bridge a place of historic importance.

The bridge, 266.5 meters in length, has 261 pillars on both sides. Carved on the pillars are 485 stone lions.

盧溝橋 （日文）

北京市西南永定河上にかかった橋。「盧溝曉月」の名で知られている。抗日戦争の発端となった1937年7月7日の「盧溝橋事変」の発生地である。だから盧溝橋はまた重大な歴史意義がある記念地である。

盧溝橋は全長266.5mで、両側に261本の「望柱」がある。柱の最上部には、歴代に彫られた485匹の獅子がある。すばらしい石彫り芸術品である。

Le Pont Lugou （法文）

Enjambant la rivière Yongding au sud-ouest de Beijing, le Pont Lugou fait l'objet de nombreux éloges pour son spectacle merveilleux dit de "Lune aurorale sur le Fossé noir". L'Incident du Pont de Lugou qui y eut lieu le 7 juillet 1937 marqua le commencement de la Guerre de résistance contre le Japon, raison pour laquelle le Pont Lugou devint un lieu commémoratif ayant une grande portée historique.

Le Pont Lugou s'étire sur 266,5 mètres. Les balustrades de ses deux côtés comptent 261 balustres ornés de 485 lions de pierre qui, réalisés à différentes époques, sont dignes d'être des chefs-d'œuvre sculpturaux en pierre.

Puente de Marco Polo （西文）

El puente llamado Lugouqiao, que atraviesa el río Yongding, al suroeste de la capital, ganó reputación por la vista que ofrece de la luna en la madrugada, razón por la que fue considerado uno de los ocho paisajes más bellos de Beijing. El 7 de Julio de 1937 ocurrió allí el acontecimiento conocido como "Incidente del Puente Lugouqiao", que marca el comienzo de la Guerra de Resistencia del Pueblo Chino contra la Invasión Japonesa y convirtió el lugar en un sitio de gran significado histórico.

De 266,5 m de largo, el puente posee en sus dos lados un total 261 pequeñas columnas sobre el balaustre, rematadas en sus extremos superiores con figuras de leones, talladas durante largo tiempo, que suman en total 485 excelentes esculturas de piedra.

Il *Lugouqiao* (Il Ponte di Marco Polo) （意大利文）

Il ponte di Marco Polo si trova a sud-ovest della capitale e attraversa il fiume Yongding. Il 7 luglio del 1937, l'incidente del ponte di Marco Polo avvenuto tra le forze

cinese e giapponese fu il preludio di un'offensiva nipponica nella Cina del Nord che portò all'occupazione di Pechino. Le fiamme contro l'aggressione giapponese che vi furono accese fecero del ponte di Marco Polo un luogo commemorativo di grande significato storico.

Si tratta di una costruzione interamente in marmo, lunga 266,5 metri, e sostenuta da undici archi ed una balaustra ornata da 261 pilastri recanti 485 leoni sulla sommità.

Die Lugou-Brücke （德文）

Die Lugou-Brücke, im Ausland als die Marco-Polo-Brücke bekannt, spannt sich über den Yongding-Fluss des Stadtbezirkes Fengtai. Sie wurde im Jahre 1189 erbaut und später mehrmals umgebaut. Die heutige Brücke ist 266,5 m lang und 7,5 m breit. An beiden Seiten dieser Steinbrücke gibt es insgesamt 280 Geländerpfosten mit 485 Steinlöwen.

Die Lugou-Brücke ist als eine historische Stätte des Zwischenfalls vom. 7. Juli 1937. An jenem Tag überfilen japanische Aggressoren die hier stationierten chinesischen Truppen. Das chinesische Volk erhob sich zum Widerstand gegen die japanischen Aggresoren.

Мост Лугоуцяо （俄文）

Мост Лугоуцяо расположен над рекой Юндинхэ, к юго-западу от Пекина.

Антияпонская война в Китае началась 7 июля 1937 года инцидентом Лугоуцяо. Это сделало этот мост памятником с историческим значением.

Длина моста – 266,5 метров. На обеих сторонах моста есть 261 столбов с 485 каменными львами, которые являются шедеврами каменных скульптур.

루거우교(蘆溝橋) （韩文）

베이징 서남쪽 융딩(永定)하에 있는 루거우교는 "노구효월(蘆溝曉月)" 풍경으로 유명하다. 1937 년 7 월 7 일 "루거우교사건" 으로 항일전생이 시작되었으며 루거우교를 중요한 역사적의의가 있는 기념지로 되게 하였다.

루거우교는 총 길이가 266.5m 이고 다리 양쪽에 기둥이 261 개 있으며 크고 작은 사자가 485 개에 달하는데 그야말로 석조각예술의 정품이라고 할 수 있다.

文化古迹——正阳门

正阳门俗称前门，是明、清两代北京城内城的正门，由城楼和箭楼两部分组成，过去城楼和箭楼由瓮城连接，1914年拆除。箭楼上下共四层，东、西、南三面墙上辟有82个箭孔。

Zhengyang Gate（英文）

The Zhengyang Gate, popularly called the Front Gate, was the main entrance to the inner city of Beijing during the Ming and Qing dynasties. It consists of the City Tower and the Watchtower, which were formerly linked by defensive enclosures. The enclosures were removed in 1914. The four-storied Watchtower has 82 loopholes in its east, west and south walls.

Das Zhengyang-Tor（德文）

Das Zhengyang-Tor, auch das Qianmen-Tor genannt, liegt am südlichen Rand des Tian'anmen-Platzes. In der Ming- und Qing-Zeit war es das Haupttor der Innenstadt Beijings. Es besteht aus dem Torturm im Norden und dem Wachtturm im Süden. Die beiden Türme waren früher durch eine Wengcheng genannte Schutzmauer miteinander verbunden. Der Torturm wurde 1421 erbaut und ist 42 m hoch. Der Wachtturm ist ein vierstöckiges Gebäude. An seiner östlichen, westlichen und südlichen Wand gibt es insgesamt 82 Schießscharten.

La Porta Zhengyang（意大利文）

Chiamata Porta Qianmen (Porta Anteriore), costituiva l'ingresso principale della città interna di Pechino durante le dinastie Ming e Qing. Composta da due parti: la Torre delle Frecce e la Torre Chenglou che in passato erano collegate alla citta interna. Nel 1914 fu smontata e poi ricostruita. La Torre della Freccia ha quattro piani. Sui muri orientale, occidentale e meridionale si trovano 82 fori da tiro di freccia.

Ворота Чжэнъянмэнь（俄文）

Обычно именуются Цяньмэнь. Являются парадным входом во внутренний городок Пекина. Чжэньянмэнь состоят из двух частей – городской башни и башни с бойницами. Связывал городскую башню и башню с бойницами полукруглая стена, которая была снесена в 1914 г. В башне с бойницами всего 4 этажа. На восточной, западной и южной стене башни – 82 бойницы для стрельбы.

Puerta Zhengyang（西文）

Conocida también como Puerta Delantera, fue la entrada principal de la ciudad interior de Beijing. Está compuesta por el castillo de base y el castillo de defensa, que se comunicaban entre sí por varias edificaciones que fueron desmanteladas en 1914. El segundo se divide en 4 pisos y en sus lados de Este, Oeste y Sur cuenta con 82 aberturas para los arqueros.

正陽門（日文）

俗は前門と称されている。明・清両代の北京城内城の表玄関。城楼と箭楼の両部分からなっている。最初は城楼と箭楼を連結する「甕城」という建物があったが、1914年に取り壊された。箭楼はあわせて4層あり、東西南の三面には82の矢を射るための「箭孔」が設けられた。

La porte Zhengyang（法文）

La porte Zhengyang (Soleil de midi), appelée aussi la porte Qianmen, était la porte principale de la ville intérieure de Beijing sous les dynasties des Ming et des Qing. Cette porte est composée d'une tour sur la muraille de la ville et d'une tour des archers, reliées autrefois par un bastion semi-circulaire, démoli en 1914. La tour des archers comprend quatre étages et ses murs est, ouest et sud portent 82 meurtrières.

정양문（韩文）

일반적으로 쳰먼(前門)이라고 하며 명·청 두 나라시기의 베이징 성내성의 정문이였으며 성루와 전루(箭樓) 두 부분으로 나뉘며 옛날에는 이 두 부분이 옹성(甕城)으로 연결되였는데 1914년에 허물어 버렸다. 전루는 모두 4층인데 동, 서, 남 세면의 벽에 82개의 화살 쏘는 구멍이 있다.

前门箭楼
The watchtower of the Front Gate
前門の箭楼
쳰먼 전루
La Tour des archers de la porte Qianmen
Der Wachtturm des Qianmen-Tors
La Porta Anteriore
Edificio de Defensa de la Puerta Delantera
Башня с бойницами ворот Цяньмэнь

文化古迹——古观象台

　　北京古观象台位于建国门南，这里在元代是大都城的东南角，元朝司天台遗址，清朝改为"观象台"，台上陈设简仪、浑仪和浑天仪等大型天文仪器，古观象台的仪器是天文科学与青铜铸造艺术完美的结合，也反映了东西方文化交流的成果。

古観象台（日文）

　　北京市建国門南部にある。もとは元（げん）が大都城の東南に建てた気象観測所「司天台」だったところで、現在の名の「観象台」は清代に改められたもの。「簡儀」、「渾儀」と「渾天儀」と称される天文観測計器が設けられてある。これらの計器は天文学知識と青銅鋳造芸術との完璧な結合であり、東西文化交流の成果である。

고 관상대（韩文）

　　베이징의 고 관상대는 젠궈먼(建國門) 남쪽에 위치해 있다. 고 관상대는 당시 원나라의 대도성의 동남쪽에 위치하였는데 원나라 사천대(司天臺)유적으로 청나라시기에 "관상대"라고 개칭하였다. 관상대에는 간의(簡儀), 혼의(渾儀)와 혼천의(渾天儀) 등 대형 천문검측의기들이 있으며 고 관상대의 의기는 천문과학과 청동제조예술의 완미한 결합이고 동서방문화교류의 성과를 반영한다.

L'Observatoire impérial （法文）

　　L'Observatoire impérial de Beijing est situé au sud de la porte Jianguo, emplacement de l'ancien observatoire des Yuan au coin sud-est de la ville de Dadu. Sous les Qing, Il reçut son nom actuel. Sur la terrasse de l'observatoire sont installés une sphère armillaire, une sphère armillaire réduite, une sphère céleste et d'autres instruments astronomiques de grande dimension. Ces instruments sont les fruits de la combinaison parfaite de la science astronomique et de la technologie de moulage du bronze, reflétant également des résultats acquis dans les échanges culturels entre la Chine et les pays occidentaux.

Ancient Observatory （英文）

　　Beijing's Ancient Observatory lies to the south of Jianguomen, formerly the southeast corner of the Yuan Dynasty's capital of Dadu. It was called the Astronomical Terrace in the Yuan Dynasty and was reconstructed into an observatory in the Qing Dynasty. The observatory houses a number of ancient astronomical instruments, including a quadrant, celestial globe and armillary sphere. These instruments demonstrate a perfect combination between astronomy and bronze casting, and they also reflect early cultural exchanges between the East and the West.

Antiguo Observatorio （西文）

　　El Antiguo Observatorio se ubica al sur de la Puerta Jianguomen, la cual pertenecía a la esquina sudeste de la Gran Capital de la dinastía Yuan. Desde entonces hasta la dinastía Qing, el lugar siempre se dedicó a la observación de las estrellas. Ahora sobre la plataforma del observatorio se exhiben los instrumentos astronómicos usados en el pasado, que además de su valor científico, ostentan un alto nivel artístico en bronce y no pocos se basaron en las tecnologías transmitidas por Occidente.

Древняя обсерватория （俄文）

　　Древняя обсерватория находится к югу от места пересечения улицы Цзяньгомэньнэйдацзе со вторым городским кольцом. В 1442 году обсерватория была построена. На обсерватории есть большие бронзовые астрономические инструменты, на которых были соединены астрономия и мастерство бронзового литья. Они отражают результаты культурных обменов между Востоком и Западом.

Osservatorio Astronomico （意大利文）

　　L'antico Osservatorio Astronomico di Pechino si trova a sud di Jianguomen che all'epoca della dinastia Yuan corrispondeva alla parte sud-orientale della città Dadu, ed era il luogo in cui si osservava il cielo. Fu chiamato Osservatorio Astronomico durante la dinastia Qing. Qui sono presenti alcuni antichi strumenti astronomici di notevole interesse quali: l'armilla abbreviata, la sfera di armilla, la teodolite ed altri ancora. Questi strumenti sono il frutto dell'unione della scienza astronomica e dell'arte della fusione del bronzo, e simboli dei rapporti di scambio e comunicazione tra la cultura orientale e quella occidentale.

Die antike Sternwarte （德文）

　　Diese Sternwarte befindet sich an der südwestlichen Ecke der Straßenüberführung bei Jianguomen des Stadtbezirkes Dongcheng. Sie wurde während der Ming-Dynastie auf der Stelle der in der Yuan-Zeit gebauten Sternwarte Sitiantai erbaut und in der folgenden Qing-Dynastie umgebaut. Heute werden hier noch acht astronomische Kupferinstrumente aus der Qing-Dynastie, darunter ein Himmelsglobus, ein Aquator- und ein Ekliptik-Theodolit sowie ein Quadrant ausgesetllt.

文化古迹——钟楼、鼓楼

北京城中轴线的北端，建有为全城击鼓报时的钟楼和鼓楼，都始建于元代（1272 年），并都于明代（1420年）重建。钟楼内有铜钟重63吨、高5.5米、直径3.4米，鼓楼内藏有整张牛皮制成的大鼓。

Bell Tower and Drum Tower （英文）

Situated on the north-south axis of Beijing, the Bell Tower and the Drum Tower were used to announce the hours in ancient times. First built in 1272, they were reconstructed in 1420 during the Ming Dynasty. The Bell Tower houses a bronze bell 63 tons in weight, 5.5 meters in height and 3.4 meters in diameter. The Drum Tower houses a huge drum made of a whole cowhide.

Der Glocken- und Trommelturm （德文）

Der Glocken- und Trommelturm befinden sich am nördlichen Rand der Zentralachse der Altstadt Beijings. Sie wurden im Jahre 1272 gebaut und im Jahre 1420 umgebaut. In beiden Türmen wurden jeweils eine Bronzeglocke und eine Trommel aufbewahrt. Die Bronzeglocke wiegt 63 Tonnen und hat eine Höhe von 5,5 m und einen Durchmeser von 3,4 m. Die Trommel ist an beiden Öffnungen mit einem Kalbfell gespannt.

Le Torri della Campana e del Tamburo （意大利文）

Le Torri della Campana e del Tamburo sono situate nella parte settentrionale lungo l'asse centrale della città di Pechino, e furonoo erette inizialmente nel 1272 durante la dinastia Yuan e ricostruite successivamente nel 1420 sotto la dinastia Ming. La campana posta nella Torre della Campana pesa 63 tonnellate ed è alta 5,5 metri con un diamentro di 3,4 metri. All'interno della Torre del Tamburo si conserva un antico tamburo di cuoio.

鐘鼓楼（日文）

北京の南北を貫く中軸線の北端にある。鐘と太鼓を叩いて時報するやり方は元に始まった。現在の鐘鼓楼は元代（1272 年）につくられたもので、明代（1420年）に建てなおされた。楼内は重さ63t、高さ5.5m、直径3.4m の銅鐘が掛かっており、太鼓は1つの牛皮を張ってつくったもの。

종·고루(鐘,鼓樓) （韩文）

베이징성의 중축선의 북쪽에 있으며 시초에 베이징성의 시간을 알리던 종루와 고루는 원나라시기（1272 년）에 건설되었고 명나라시기（1420 년）에 재건하였다. 종루에는 무게가 63ton, 높이가 55m, 직경이 34m 인 구리종이 걸려있다. 고루에는 한장의 완전한 소가죽으로 만든 큰 북이 있다.

La Tour de la Cloche et la Tour du Tambour （法文）

La Tour de la Cloche et la Tour du Tambour, situées à l'extrémité nord de l'axe central de Beijing, servant jadis à donner l'heure à toute la ville par le battement du tambour, furent construites en 1272 sous les Yuan et reconstruites en 1420 sous les Ming. La Tour de la Cloche abrite une cloche de bronze de 5,5 mètres de haut et de 3,4 mètres de diamètre, pesant 63 tonnes, tandis que dans la Tour du Tambour est conservé un grand tambour fait de la peau d'un buffle.

Edificios de la Campana y el Tambor （西文）

En el extremo norte del eje central de Beijing, se sitúan los Edificios de la Campaña y el Tambor, que se encargaban de dar a conocer la hora mediante campanadas y tamborileos. Se construyeron por primera vez en tiempos de la dinastía Yuan – año 1272- y pasaron por una restauración en 1420, cuando gobernaba la dinastía Ming. La campana de bronce pesa 63 toneladas y mide 5,5 m. de alto y 3,4 m. de diámetro. El tambor se hizo con un gran pedazo de piel de buey.

Колокольня и барабанная башня （俄文）

Находятся на севере Пекина. Были построены в 1272 г. и реконструированы в 1420 г. Они работали для поверки времени. В башне колокола есть медный колокол, весом 63 тонны, высотой 5,5 метров, диаметром 3,4 метров. В башне барабана сохранился крупный барабан, сделанный из целостной коровьей кожи.

鼓楼　鼓楼　고루
The Drum Tower
La Tour du Tambour
Der Trommelturm
Torre del Tamburo
Edificio del Tambor
Башня барабана

文化古迹——国子监、孔庙

孔庙位于国子监街，是元、明、清三代祭祀中国战国末期著名思想家、教育家和儒家学说创始人孔子的地方。

与孔庙相邻的是管理教育的行政机构和最高学府国子监。

Confucius Temple and Imperial Academy（英文）

Located on Guozijian Street, the Confucius Temple was used to worship Confucius, a renowned thinker and educator of the late Warring States Period (475-221BC) and founder of Confucianism, during the Yuan, Ming and Qing dynasties.

Adjacent to the Confucius Temple is the Imperial Academy, the supreme educational center in ancient times.

Le Temple de Confucius et le Collège impérial（法文）

Situé dans la rue de Guozijian, le Temple de Confucius était le lieu où on vénérait Confucius, célèbre penseur, pédagogue et fondateur du confucianisme de la fin des Royaumes combattants (475 – 221 av. J.-C.), sous les Yuan, les Ming et les Qing.

A côté du Temple de Confucius, c'est l'ancien Collège impérial, école supérieure et siège de l'organisme d'administration de l'éducation sous les dynasties féodales.

Il Tempio di Confucio e il Collegio Imperiale（意大利文）

Situato lungo la via Guozijian, il Tempio di Confucio era il luogo dei sacrifici a Confucio, famoso pensatore, educatore che visse all'epoca degli Stati Combattenti e fondò l'importantissima dottrina del Confucianesimo. Il Colleggio Imperiale era il luogo in cui l'imperatore, una volta l'anno, spiegava i classici confuciani a un uditorio di migliaia di studenti, professori e funzionari di corte che ascoltavano inginocchiati.

Templo de Confucio e Instituto Imperial（西文）

Situado en la actual calle Guozijian, durante las tres dinastías, Yuan, Ming y Qing, fue el lugar donde se realizaron los ritos de veneración en honor a Confucio, famoso filósofo y pedagogo nacido en las postrimerías de la época de los Estados Combatientes.

Contiguo al templo, se encuentra el Instituto Imperial, que en el pasado fue el centro de enseñanza superior y a la vez el departamento administrativo de la enseñanza.

孔子廟と国子監（日文）

孔子廟は国子監街にある。元、明、清三代が戦国末期の著名な思想家、教育家と儒家学説の創立者・孔子を祭ったところである。

孔子廟と隣り合わしている国子監は教育を管理する最高機関と最高学府である。

孔子像
A Statue of Confucius
孔子像
공자상
Portrait de Confucius
Porträt von Konfuzius
Il ritratto di Confucio
Retrato de Confucio
Статуя Конфуция

Der Konfuzius-Tempel und Guozijian（德文）

Der Konfuzius-Tempel liegt an der Guozijian-Straße des Stadtbezirkes Dongcheng. Er wurde während der Yuan-Dynastie zur Erinnerung an Konfizius, den großen Philosphen, Pädagogen und den Begründer des Konfuzianismus aus der späteren Zeit der der Streitenden Reiche, erbaut und in den folgenden Dynastien Ming und Qing mehrmals umgebaut.

Bei Guozijian handelt es sich um die kaiserliche Akademie und auch die höchste kaiserliche Lehranstalt der Dynastien Yuan, Ming und Qing. Sie liegt in der Nähe des Konfuzius-Tempels.

Храм Конфуция и Гоцзыцзянь (государственное училище)（俄文）

Является местом, где юаньские, минские и цинские императоры приносили жертву Конфуцию.

Рядом храма находится наивысшее государственное училище и орган, управляющий образованием – Гоцзыцзянь.

공자묘, 국자감（韩文）

공자묘는 귀쯔젠거리에 위치해 있으며 원·명·청 세 나라시기 중국 전국시기의 유명한 사상가, 교육가, 유교학설의 창시인인 공자를 기념하는 곳이다.

공자묘와 이웃하고 있는 것은 중국 고대 교육관리의 행정기구이며 최고 학부인 국자감이다.

文化古迹——太庙、社稷坛

太庙位于天安门东侧，明、清两代皇家祭祖的地方。太庙大殿的建筑规格是皇家的最高等级。

社稷坛位于天安门右侧，与东边的太庙一左一右，体现了"左祖右社"设计原则。社稷坛是用来供奉和祭祀社神和稷神的。

Temple of the Imperial Ancestors （英文）

Situated to the east of the Tian'anmen Rostrum, the Temple of Imperial Ancestors was where the Ming and Qing emperors worshipped their ancestors. Its main hall represents the supreme level of imperial architecture.

Altar of Earth and Grain

The Altar of Earth and Harvest is situated to the right of the Tian'anmen Rostrum, to the left of which stands the Temple of the Imperial Ancestors. Such a layout demonstrates the traditional concept of "Ancestors on the left and Earth on the right." The altar was used to worship the god of earth and grain.

太廟（労働人民文化宮）（日文）

天安門の東側にある。明・清両代の皇帝が祖先を祭ったところである。太廟内の本殿は皇室建築においても最高等級のものである。

社稷壇（中山公園）

天安門右側にある。東側の太廟（労働人民文化宮）とは対称するように配置されている。封建時代の「左祖先右社稷」の原則に従ったもの。社稷壇は社稷と社稷の神を祭る場所である。

태묘(노동인민문화궁) （韓文）

톈안먼의 동쪽에 있으며 명·청 두 나라의 황제가 조상을 기념하는 곳이다. 태묘 대전(大殿)의 건축규모는 황가의 최고 등급이다.

사직단(중산공원)

톈안먼의 오른쪽에 위치하여 있으며 동쪽의 태묘와 함께 하나는 왼쪽, 하나는 오른쪽에 위치하여 "좌조우사(左祖右社)"의 설계원칙을 나타내었다. 사직단은 사신 (社神)과 직신(稷神)을 모시는 곳이다.

Le Temple des ancêtres (Palais de la Culture des Travailleurs) （法文）

Situé à l'est de la porte Tian An Men, le Temple des ancêtres (Taimiao) était l'endroit où les empereurs des Ming et des Qing venaient vénérer leurs ancêtres. La Salle des ancêtres fut réalisée selon le critère d'architecture impérial le plus exigeant.

L'Autel du Sol et des Moissons

L'Autel du Sol et des Moissons (Shejitan) est situé à l'ouest de la porte Tian An Men, faisant symétrie avec le Temple des ancêtres à l'est de la même porte. Cette disposition a traduit la conception des Chinois selon laquelle les ancêtres sont à gauche et le Dieu de la Terre est à droite. Cet autel était l'endroit où l'empereur offrait les sacrifices au Dieu de la Terre et au Dieu des Cinq céréales.

Templo Ancestral Imperial (Palacio Cultural de los Trabajadores) （西文）

Enclavado al este de la Puerta Tian´anmen, el templo se empleaba en las ceremonias en las que se ofrecían sacrificios a los antepasados de la casa real, por eso su pabellón principal ostenta la suprema jerarquía entre todas las edificaciones.

Altar de la Tierra y el Grano (Parque Zhongshan)

A la izquierda y la derecha de la Puerta Tian´anmen se sitúan el Templo Ancestral Imperial y el Altar de la Tierra y el Grano, respectivamente, distribución establecida en respeto a la tradición china. Originalmente el altar se dedicó a los dioses de la tierra y el grano.

Der kaiserliche Ahnentempel (Kulturpalast der Werktätigen) （德文）

Er liegt an der östlichen Seite des Tian'anmen-Tors. Während der Ming- und Qing-Dynastie hieß er Taimiao (Ahnentempel der kaiserlichen Familie). Das Haupgebäude des Tempels ist die Große Halle.

Der Sheji-Altar (Sun-Yat-sen-Park)

Der Shi-Altar befindet sich im Westen des Tian'anmen-Tors. Zur Zeit der Ming- und Qing-Dynastie kamen die Kaiser hierher, um den Gott der Erde und die Götter der fünf Getreidearten für eine reiche Ernte anzubeten.

Il Tempio degli Antenati Imperiali (Parco della Cultura del Popolo) （意大利文）

Il parco della Cultura del Popolo si estende a est della porta di Tian'anmen (della Pace Celeste). Inizialmente era in gran parte occupato dal Taimiao (tempio degli Antenati Imperiali). Questo edificio rappresentava il più elevato edificio, in termini di importanza, nel sistema dell'architettura imperiale.

L'Altare della Terra e delle Messi (Parco Sun Yat-sen)

Il parco Sun Yat-sen si trova a destra della porta di Tian'anmen (della Pace Celeste) e lungo il lato settentrionale confina con il fossato di protezione della Città Proibita. L'Altare della Terra e delle Messi fu eretto al suo interno e qui, due volte l'anno gli imperatori compivano sacrifici alle divinità dei campi e dell'agricoltura.

Храм императорских предков (ныне Дворец культуры трудящихся) （俄文）

Находится на востоке от ворот Тяньаньмэнь. Здесь минские и цинские императоры приносили жертву предкам. Главный зал храма был построен по стандарту наивысшей степени императорского дома.

Алтарь Шэцзитань (парк имени Сунь Ятсена)

Находится на западе от ворот Тяньаньмэнь. На алтаре Шэцзитань приносили жертву и божествам земли и злаков.

文化古迹——天宁寺、白塔寺

天宁寺为北魏（471～475年）时创建。经隋、唐到辽代在寺后院建塔。天宁寺塔八角十三级，总高57.8米，距今900余年。

白塔寺始建于元至元十六年（1279年），院内有1271年建的藏式白色喇嘛塔，俗称白塔寺。为元大都的宗教、政治、文化举足轻重之地。

Tianning Temple and White Dagoda Temple （英文）

Tianning Temple was first built in the Northern Wei Dynasty (471-475). During the Liao Dynasty (907-1125), an octagonal dagoda was erected in its rear courtyard. The 57.8-meter-high pagoda has 13 stories.

First built in 1279, the 16th year of the Zhiyuan reign of the Yuan Dynasty, the White Dagoda Temple houses a Tibetan-style white dagoda that was constructed in 1271, hence its name. It occupied an important position in religion, politics and culture during the Yuan Dynasty.

天寧寺、白塔寺 （日文）

天寧寺は北魏(西暦471～475年)に建立された仏寺で、隋、唐をへて遼の時に高さ57.8mの八角形13層の塔が増築された。今日まではすでに900余年の歴史がある。

元の至元十六年(1279年)に建てられたもので、境内には西暦1271年に建てたチベットスタイルの白色ラマ塔がある。白塔寺の名はそれにちなんだもの。元の大都における大切な宗教、政治、文化建築である。

톈닝사(天寧寺)，바이타사 (白塔寺) （韩文）

톈닝사는 북위시기[北魏](471~475년)부터 수·당·요나라 시기까지 절의 뒷 마당에 탑을 건축하였다. 톈닝사의 탑은 팔각십삼급이고 높이가 57.8m이고 900여 년의 역사를 가지고 있다.

원나라 때 16년에 걸쳐 1279년에 준공되었다. 사찰에는 1271년에 건설한 흰색의 티베트식 라마탑이 있기 때문에 이름을 바이타사라고 하였다. 원나라 대도의 종교, 정치, 문화에서 중요한 작용을 일으켰던 곳이다.

Храм Тяньнинсы–Храм Байтасы （俄文）

Храм Тяньнинсы был построен в династии Бэйвэй (471-475г). В династии Ляо в заднем дворе храма была возведена восьмиугольная пагода с 13 ступнями. Высота пагоды – 57,8 метров. Она уже существует более 900 лет.

Строительство храма началось с 1279 г. Во дворе храма есть белая ламаиская пагода. Храм является важным местом религиозной, политической и культурной жизни юаньской столицы.

Il Tempio della Pace Celeste, Il tempio della Pagoda Bianca （意文）

Lungo la via Guang'anmenwai Beibihelu, nella zona sudoccidentale di Pechino, si trova il Tianningsi, santuario buddhista un tempo molto famoso. Si tratta di una costruzione del V secolo risalente alla dinastia dei Wei Settentrionali (471-475), che fu più volte distrutta e ricostruita: del primo periodo è ancora visibile una pagoda in pietra della dinastia Liao (907-1125) alta 57,8 metri e di ben tredici piani, uno degli edifici più antichi della città che vanta 900 anni di storia e uno dei più importanti tipi di pagoda.

Il tempio della Pagoda Bianca, costruito nel 1279, prende nome dalla struttra in stile tibetano che fu eretta nel 1271. Fu un luogo importante per la capitale Dadu della dinastia Yuan per motivi religiosi, politici e culturali.

Der Tianning-Tempel, der Baita-Tempel （德文）

Der Tianning-Tempel liegt bei Guang'anmen des Stadtbezirkes Xuanwu. Er wurde schon in der Zeit der Nördlichen Wei-Dynastie (471—475) gebaut und später mehrmals umgebaut. Heute sieht hier man noch eine 57,8 m hohe Pagode aus Ziegelsteinen. Sie wurde während der Liao-Dynastie erbaut und hat also eine Geschichte von mehr als 900 Jahren.

Der Baita-Tempel, auch Miaoying-Tempel genannt, liegt an der nördliche Seite der Straße Fuchengmennei des Stadtbezirkes Xicheng. Er wurde im Jahre 1279 gebaut. Im Tempelhof liegt eine 50,9 m hohe weiße Pagode im lamaistischen Baustil. Sie wurde im Jahre 1271 gebaut.

Le Temple de la Sérénité céleste Le Temple du Dagoba blanc （法文）

Le Temple de la Sérénité céleste (Tianningsi) fut créé sous les Wei du Nord (471 – 475) et sous les Liao, une pagode fut construite dans sa cour de derrière. D'un tronc octogonal et comprenant 13 niveaux, cette pagode mesure 57,8 mètres de haut et a déjà plus de 900 ans d'histoire.

La construction du Temple du Dagoba blanc (Baitasi) débuta en l'An 16 du règne Zhiyuan (1279) de l'empereur Shundi des Yuan. En 1271, on y construisit un dagoba blanc de style tibétain, ce qui lui vaut son nom actuel. Ce temple a joué un rôle capital dans les domaines religieux, politique et culturel sous les Yuan.

Templo Tianning y Templo de la Pagoda Blanca （西文）

El templo budista Tianning se construyó del año 471 al 475, en tiempos de la dinastía Wei del Norte. En la dinastía Liao, se erigió en su patio trasero una pagoda octágona de 13 pisos y 57,8 m. de alto, que cuenta ya con más de 900 años.

El nombre del segundo tegundo templo se deriva de la pagoda blanca erigida en 1271, de típico estilo tibetano. La construcción del resto del monasterio se inició en 1279, a comienzos de la dinastía Yuan, a lo largo de la cual desempeñó un importante papel religioso, político y cultural en la Gran Capital.

潭柘寺

始建于晋代（265～316年），是北京地区最早的一座寺院，有"先有潭柘寺，后有幽州（北京）城"之说。寺周九峰环列，背依宝珠峰，称之为"九龙戏珠"。潭柘寺一直地位显赫，香火长盛不衰。

Tanzhe Temple（英文）

First built in the Jin Dynasty (265-316), Tanzhe Temple is the oldest Buddhist temple in Beijing. It is said that "First there was the Tanzhe Temple, then there was Youzhou (present-day Beijing)." Nestling against Baozhu Peak, the temple is embraced by nine peaks, and the layout is called "Nine Dragons Playing with a Pearl." Due to its prominent position in Buddhism, the temple has attracted numerous pilgrims.

탄저사(潭柘寺)（韩文）

진나라시기(265~316년)에 시작하여 건설하였으며 베이징 지역 최초의 절묘한 경관에 속하며 "먼저 탄저사가 있고 나중에 베이징성이 있었다." 라고 전해지고 있다. 사찰의 주위에는 아홉개의 봉우리가 있고 뒤에는 보주(寶珠)봉이 있어 "구용희주(九龍嬉珠)"로 불리우고 있다. 탄저사는 시민들 속에서 혁혁한 지위를 가지고 있으며 향불이 줄곧 꺼지지 않고 있다.

Le Temple de la Mare et du Mûrier（法文）

Créé sous la dynastie des Jin (265 – 316), le Temple de la Mare et du Mûrier (Tanzhesi) est le plus vieux temple de la région de Beijing. On dit que le Temple de la Mare et du Mûrier est plus ancien que Youzhou (Beijing). Il est entouré de neuf monts et adossé au mont Baozhu. On qualifie cette situation géographique de "neuf dragons jouant avec une perle". Le Temple de la Mre et su Mûrier occupe toujours une place importante et les pèlerins s'y rendent à flots.

Der Tanzhe-Tempel（德文）

Der Tanzhe-Tempel liegt am Abhang des Tanzhe-Berges des Stadtbezirkes Mentougou. Er wurde während der Westlichen Jin-Dynastie (265—316) gebaut. Damit ist er der älteste Sakralbau Beijings. So gibt es in Beijing eine Redeart über das Alter dieses Tempels: „Zuerst entstand der Tanzhe-Tempel, hernach die Stadt Beijing." Bis heute zieht dieser Tempel noch viele Pilger an.

Templo Tanzhe（西文）

Data de la dinastía Jin (265-316) y es el templo budista más antiguo en la zona de Beijing, de ahí el refrán popular "Apareció primero el Templo Tanzhe y luego la ciudad de Beijing". Se apoya en la Colina de Perla y está rodeado por nueve picos, ubicación descrita como "Juego de perla de los nueve dragones". Pese al tiempo transcurrido, nunca ha perdido su posición eminente y cada día recibe un gran número de visitantes.

Il tempio Tanzhe（意大利文）

L'inizio della sua costruzione risalirebbe agli anni compresi tra il 265 e il 316. Fu il primo santuario edificato nella zona di Pechino per cui esiste il detto che prima fu edificato il Tanzhesi e quindi la città di Youzhou (uno degli antichi nomi di Pechino). Circondato da nove colline allineate e dalla collina Baozhu che si trova dietro al Tanzhesi, per questo è anche chiamato "I nove draghi che giocano con la perla". Il Tanzhesi fu un imponente santuario molto frequentato in cui giungevano numerosi pellegrini ogni anno.

Храм Таньчжэсы（俄文）

Был построен в династии Цзинь (265-316 г.). Является самым древним храмом в районе Пекина. Среди пекинцев ходит молва, что Пекин был построен после сооружения храма Таньчжэсы. Вокруг храма – 9 горы. Это называется «игра 9 драконов с жемчужиной». В истории Китая Таньчжэсы занимал важное политическое, экономическое, культурное и религиозное место.

潭柘寺（日文）

晋代(265~316年)に建立された仏寺。北京地域においては、歴史があまりにも長いため、「先ず潭柘寺があり、後に幽州(北京)城がある」の説さえある。周辺は9つの峰に取り囲まれ、宝珠峰を背にしている。これは「玉と戯れる9匹の竜」と呼んでいる。地位が高くお参りが盛んである。

云居寺、法源寺

云居寺始建于隋大业年间（605～618年）规模宏大，历史悠久，保存了自隋末至清初十一个世纪中完成的共14278块石刻经版，共刻有900多部3452卷经文，堪称"世界之最"。

法源寺是北京城内现存寺院中历史最悠久的名刹。为唐太宗李世民为阵亡将士建的寺。

雲居寺 法源寺（日文）

隋の大業年間(605~618年)に建立された規模が大きく、歴史が古い仏寺である。寺内は隋末から清初までの1100年間に刻された1万4278枚の石刻経版版が保存され、全部で900部3452巻の経文に及んでいる。世界のトップである。

北京市内に現存する歴史がもっとも古い名刹である。唐の太宗・李世民が戦死将士を記念するために建てたもの。

Der Dazhong-Tempel（德文）

Der Dazhong-Tempel, auch der Juesheng-Tempel genannt, liegt an der nördlichen Seite der Bei'erhuan-Straße des Stadtbeszirkes Haidian. Hier wird eine riesige Glocke aufbewahrt. Sie wurde während der Yongle-Regierungsperiode der Ming-Dynastie gegossen, ist 6,75 m hoch, wiegt 46,5 Tonnen und hat einen Durchmesser von 3,3 m. An der Innen- und Außenseite der Glocke befinden sich verschiedene Sutren mit insgesamt 230 000 chinesischen Schriftzeichen.

Il Tempio della Grande Campana （意大利文）

Nel tempio si conserva una grande campana in bronzo fusa durante il periodo del regno dell'imperatore Yongle della dinastia Ming: alta 6,75 metri con un diametro di 3,3 metri e pesa 4,6 tonnellate. Sulla superficie sia interna che esterna della campana è riportato il testo completo di un sutra buddista, che ha appunto dato il nome alla campana e comprende oltre 230.000 ideogrammi cinesi e caratteri in lingua sanscrita.

Храм Дачжунсы （俄文）

В храме сохранился большой колокол «Юнлэ», отлитый в династии Мин. Высота колокола – 6,75 метров, диаметр – 3,3 метров, вес – 93000 цзинь (цзинь – половина килограммы). На всем колоколе были вырезаны 8 канонов на китайском языке, и сутры на китайском и санскрите, длиной 230 тыс. с лишним метров. Этот колокол еще имеет другое название–«царь древних колоколов».

Templo de la Gran Campana （西文）

En él hay una colosal campana fundida en los años Yongle, de la dinastía Ming, que mide 6,75 m. de alto y 3,3 m. de diámetro y pesa 46.500 Kg. En su superficie aparecen grabadas las inscripciones de ocho sutras y los conjuros en idioma chino e hindú, que totalizan más de 230.000 m. de largo, de ahí su fama como Reina de las Campanas.

智化寺

智化寺始建于明正统8年（1443年），智化寺保留了原汁原味的明代宫廷音乐，未加变动地密传了28代。

Zhihua Temple （英文）

Built in 1443, the 8th year of the Zhengtong reign period of the Ming Dynasty, the Zhihua Temple preserves the ritual music of the Ming court, which has been handed down for 28 generations.

智化寺 （日文）

明の正統八年(1443年)に建立された仏寺。28代も続いた秘伝の明代宮廷音楽の演奏はこの寺の十八番。

즈화사(智化寺)（韩文）

즈화사(지화사)는 명나라 정통8년(1443년)부터 건설하였다. 즈화사는 명나라 궁정음악을 그대로 보존하고 있으며 그대로 고스란이 28대까지 전해졌으며 "삼방문물(三方文物)"으로 불리고 있다.

Le Temple de la Sagesse （法文）

Créé en l'An 8 du règne Zhengtong (1443) de l'empereur Yingzong des Ming, le Temple de la Sagesse (Zhihuasi) conserve des morceaux de musique de la cour impériale des Ming, qui ont été transmis inchangés de la première génération jusqu'à la vingt-huitième.

Der Zhihua-Tempel （德文）

Der Zhihua-Tempel liegt bei Lümicang des Stadtbezirkes Dongcheng und wurde im Jahre 1443 erbaut. Der Tempel zeichnet sich durch die typische Kammermusik der Ming-Dynastie aus, die seit 28 Generationen hier bewahrt wird.

Il Tempio dell'Acquisizione della Saggezza （意大利文）

Costruito nel 1443 durante la dinastia Ming, il Tempio dell'Acquisizione della Saggezza ha conservato le musiche della corte imperiale Ming.

Храм Чжихуасы （俄文）

Был построен в 1443 г. Здесь сохранилась чистая минская дворцовая музыка, которая уже передается без изменения до 28-ого поколения.

Templo Zhihua （西文）

En esta construcción de 1443, años Zhengtong de la dinastía Ming, el mayor tesoro es la música original imperial de la corte Ming, que se trasmitió secretamente durante 28 generaciones y mantiene intacto su encanto.

雍和宫

雍和宫是北京城内规模最大的喇嘛庙。原是清雍亲王府。雍和宫法轮殿中的五百罗汉山，照佛楼里的金丝楠木佛龛、万福阁里整棵白檀木雕成的28米高的弥勒佛像，被誉为雍和宫的三绝。

Lama Temple（英文）

Originally the Mansion of Prince Yong, the Lama Temple is the largest Tibetan Buddhist temple in Beijing. The 500-Arhat Hill in the Hall of Wheel of the Law, the *phoebe nanmu* niche in the Hall of the Shining Buddha and the 28-meter-tall statue of the Buddha Maitreya carved out of a single piece of white sandalwood are collectively called the Three Wonders of the Lama Temple.

Templo de los Lamas（西文）

Originalmente fue la residencia del príncipe Aisin Gioro Yinzhen, pero luego se convirtió en la mayor lamasería de Beijing. La Montaña de los quinientos arhats, en el Salón de la Rueda de la Ley, el nicho en madera del árbol nanmu, en el Edificio del Reflejo de Buda, y la estatua de Meitreya, de 28m de alto, esculpida en un sándalo blanco entero, del Salón de las Diez Mil Felicidades, conforman las tres excelencias de las reliquias conservadas en su interior.

Le Palais de l'Eternelle Harmonie（法文）

Le Palais de l'Eternelle Harmonie (Yonghegong) est le plus grand temple lamaïste dans la ville de Beijing. C'était à l'origine la résidence du prince Yong qui devint plus tard l'empereur Yongzheng des Qing. Le Mont des Cinq Cents Arhats de la Salle de la Roue de la Loi (Falundian), la niche de bouddha fait de *Machilus Nanmu* du Pavillon du Bouddha illuminé (Zhaofolou) et l'immense statue en pied de Maitreya mesurant 28 mètres de haut, sculptée dans un tronc de santal, sont connus pour être les "Trois Merveilles" du Palais de l'Eternelle Harmonie.

Yonghegong（德文）

Es handelt sich dabei um den größten lamaistischen Tempel Beijings. Er liegt an der östlichen Seite der Yonghegong-Straße des Stadtbezirkes Dongcheng. Früher diente er als die Residenz des Qing-Kaisers Yong Zhong vor seiner Thronbesteigung. Von seinen zahlreichen kostbaren Kulturgegenstände sind der „Berg der 500 Archats" in der Falun-Halle, die 28 m hohe Maitreja-Statue (die aus einem Sandelbaumstamm geschntitz wurde) im Wanfu-Pavillon und die Buddha-Nische aus Nanmu-Holz in der Zhaofo-Halle am bekanntesten.

Lo Yonghegong (Palazzo dell'Eterna Armonia meglio conosciuto come Tempio del Lama)（意大利文）

Lo Yonghegong è il maggiore tempio lamaista presente nella città di Pechino. Originariamente esso fu la residenza del principe Yong della dinastia Qing. Al suo interno vi sono numerose statue scolpite in legno e in bronzo fra cui: i cinquecento arhat nella Falundian (Sala della Ruota della Legge), il Buddha in bronzo assiso su una pedana in prezioso legno nella sala Zhaofolou e la statua di Maitreya alta 28 metri di sandalo tibetano bianco, ricavata da un unico tronco dal diametro di 3 metri, conservata nella sala Wanfuge ritenuti fra i migliori nello Yonghegong.

Храм Юньхэгун（俄文）

Является самым крупным и великолепным ламаистским монастырем в Пекине. Свою историю Юнхэгуна ведет с 1694 году, когда китайский император Канси построил здесь дворец для своего сына Юн-цинвана. Изваяния 500 Лоханей в павильоне Фалунцзянь, киоты из махила в павильоне Чжаофолоу и 28-метровая статуя Будды будущего – Майтрейн в павильоне Ваньфугэ, вырезанная из единого ствола сандалового дерева широко известны в Китае.

雍和宫（日文）

北京市内最大規模のラマ廟である。最初は清の雍親王の邸宅であった。その法輪殿内の五百羅漢山、照仏楼内のくすのきで彫った仏龕と万福閣内のビャクダンの木で彫った高さ28mの弥勒仏の影像は、雍和宮の3種絶品と称えられている。

융허궁(雍和宮)（韩文）

융허궁(옹화궁)은 베이징성에서 규모가 가장 큰 라마 묘이다. 본래는 청나라의 옹친왕의 거처였다. 융허궁의 법륜전(法輪殿)의 500명 나한(羅漢)으로 이루어진 나한산, 조불누(照佛樓)의 금사 녹나무불감, 만복각(萬福閣)의 백참빛살나무로 조각한 26m 높이의 미륵블상은 융허궁의 삼대 절묘한 풍경이다.

雍和宫大佛
Grand Buddha Statue
雍和宫大仏
옹화궁의 대불
Le Grand Bouddh du Palais de l'Eternelle Harmonie.
Die Große Buddhafigur, im Lamatempel Yonghegong aufbewahrt
Un gigante buddha conservato nel Tempio lamaista
Большой Будда в храме Юнхэгунь
Gran Buda del Templo de los Lamas

白云观

坐落于北京西便门外的白云观，不仅是北京最大的道观，而且是中国古代北方道教的中心。创建于739年（唐玄宗开元二十七年），有"全真龙门派第一丛林"之称。

White Cloud Temple（英文）

The White Cloud Temple, located near Xibianmen, is the largest Taoist temple in Beijing. Built in 739, the 27th year of the Kaiyuan reign period of the Tang Dynasty, it is the No.1 sanctum of the Complete Perfection Sect of Taoism, and north China's most important Taoist shrine in ancient times.

白雲観（日文）

北京市西便門外にある北京最大の道教寺と中国の北方における道教の中心地である。唐の玄宗・開元二十七年(西暦739年)に建立されたもの。「全真竜門派第一の叢林(道教寺の別名)」の称がある。

바이윈관（白雲觀）（韩文）

베이징의 시몐문(西便) 밖에 있는 바이윈관은 베이징 최대 도교 사찰이며 중국 고대 도교의 중심지이다. 739년(당현종 개원 27 년)에 건설되었으며 "전진용문(全眞龍門)의 제일 사원"으로 불리고 있다.

Даосский храм Байюньгуань（俄文）

Находится на улице Сибяньмэнвай. Является крупнейшим даосским храмом и в древности он был центром даосизма на севере Китая. В 739 году был построен данный храм.

Le Temple taoïste des Nuages blancs（法文）

Situé en dehors de la porte Xibianmen de Beijing, le Temple taoïste des Nuages blancs (Baiyunguan) est le plus grand temple des taoïstes de Beijing, ancien centre du taoïsme en Chine du Nord. Créé en 739 (l'An 27 du règne Kaiyuan de l'empereur Xuanzong des Tang), était réputé pour être le premier temple de l'Ecole de la Vérité complète du taoïsme.

Templo Taoísta Baiyunguan（西文）

Situado fuera del barrio Xibianmen, Baiyunguan es el mayor templo taoísta de Beijing. Fue construido en 739, 27mo año del periodo Kaiyuan del emperador Xuanzong, de la dinastía Tang. Mantuvo su posición central en el norte chino en la antigüedad y fue bautizado como Templo No. 1 de la secta de la Realidad Completa.

Baiyunguan（德文）

Baiyunguan, außerhalb des Xibianmen-Tors des Stadtbezirkes Xicheng gelegen, ist der größte taoistische Tempel Beijings. Er wurde im Jahre 739 während der Tang-Dynastie erbaut und diente als das taoistische Zentrum Nordchinas. Heute ist Baiyunguan als eine heilige Stätte der Quanzhen-Sekte des Taoismus bekannt.

Il Tempio della Nuvola Bianca（意大利文）

Il Tempio della Nuvola Bianca, situato lungo la via Xibianmenwai di Pechino è il più grande tempio taoista della capitale, nonché centro del taoismo della Cina settentrionale antica. Fu costruito nel 739 (27º anno del regno dell'imperatore Xuanzong della dinastia Tang).

牛街礼拜寺

牛街礼拜寺始建于辽统和十四年（996年）。是北京最古老的伊斯兰古寺，其建筑为中国传统的砖木结构和伊斯兰教细部装饰相结合的独特风格。该寺在国内外享有盛誉。

Niujie Mosque（英文）

Built in 996, the 14th year of the Tonghe reign period of the Liao Dynasty, this is the oldest mosque in Beijing. Well-known both at home and abroad, the mosque combines traditional Chinese architectural style with Muslim detailed decorations.

牛街礼拝寺（日文）

遼の統和十四年(西暦996年)に建立された北京地域最古のイスラム教寺。建物には中国の伝統的な構造とイスラム教建築の細緻な装飾を結びつける特徴がある。国内外に名が知られるイスラム教寺である。

La Mosquée de Niujie（法文）

Fondée en l'An 14 du règne Tonghe (996) de l'empereur Shengzong des Liao, la Mosquée de Niujie (rue des Bœufs) est la mosquée la plus ancienne de Beijing. Ses édifices combinent la structure d'architecture traditionnelle chinoise et la décoration islamique. Cette mosquée est aussi réputée en Chine qu'à l'étranger.

Mezquita en la calle Niujie（西文）

Data del 996, 14to año del reinado Tonghe, de la dinastía Liao, y es la mezquita más antigua en Beijing. Goza de alta fama dentro y fuera del país. Su construcción combina la estructura tradicional de China y los adornos de carácter musulmán.

La Moschea Niujie (della Via dei Buoi)（意大利文）

Costruita nel 996, la Moschea Niujie è la più antica del suo genere a Pechino. La sua architettura combina lo stile tradizionale dell'architettura cinese con la decorazione tipica islamica.

Die Niujie-Moschee（德文）

Die Niujie-Moschee liegt an der gleichnamigen Straße des Stadtbezirkes Xuanwu. Sie wurde im Jahre 996 erbaut und ist damit die älteste und größte Moschee Beijings. Sie weist einen chinesischen und islamischen Baustil auf. Heute ist die Niujie-Moschee auch im Ausland sehr bekannt.

Мечеть на улице Нюцзе（俄文）

Был построен в 996 году. Является самым древним мусульманским храмом в Пекине. Архитектура этой мечети отличается соединением традиционной китайской структуры с мусульманским декоративным искусством. Эта мечеть прославляется и в Китае и за рубежом.

뉴제리바이사(牛街禮拜寺)（韩文）

요나라 통화(統和) 14년(996년)에 건설되었다. 이것은 북경에서 가장 오랜 이슬람교 사원이며 중국 전통 건축 구조와 이슬람교의 세부적인 장식의 조합으로서 독특한 건축품격을 가지고 있다. 이 사찰는 국내외에서 아주 유명하다.

天主教南堂

天主教南堂位于宣武门东北，始建于明万历三十三年（1605年）先后由意大利传教士利马窦和德国传教士汤若望修建。

South Cathedral（英文）

Situated to the northeast of Xuanwumen, this catholic cathedral was built in 1650, the 33rd year of the Wanli reign period of the Ming Dynasty. Italian priest Matteo Ricci and German missionary Johann Adam Schall von Bell presided over its construction.

天主教南堂（日文）

北京市宣武門東北にある。明の万暦三十三年（1605年）ころ、イタリア人宣教師マテオリッチとドイツ人宣教師アダム・チャールによって建立されたキリスト教会である。

L'Eglise catholique du Sud（法文）

Située au nord-est de l'ancienne porte Xuanwu, cette église date de l'An 33 du règne Wanli (1605) de l'empereur Shenzong des Ming. Elle fut construite pour la première fois par le missionnaire italien P. Matteo Ricci et puis par le jésuite allemand Adam Schall.

Die südliche katholische Kirche（德文）

Diese Kirche liegt vor dem ehemaligen Xuanwumen-Tor des Stadtbezirkes Xuanwu im Süden Beijings. Sie wurde im Jahre 1605 während der Ming-Dynastie unter Leitung des italienischen Missionars Matteo Ricci erbaut und später unter der Leitung des deutschen Missionars Johan Adam Schall von Bell umgebaut.

Iglesia Católica del Sur（西文）

En 1605, 33er año del reinado Wanli, de la dinastía Ming, bajo la dirección del misionero italiano Matteo Ricci y luego del misionero alemán Joannes Adam Schall von Bell, se inició la construcción de la iglesia, que se sitúa al noreste de la Puerta Xuanwu.

La Chiesa cattolica Meridionale（意大利文）

La Chiesa Meridionale si trova nella parte nord-orientale di Xuanwumen. Costruita nel 1605 (XXXIII anno del regno dell'imperatore Wanli della dinastia Ming) fu successivamente ricostruita rispettivamente dal missionario cattolico italiano Matteo Ricci e dal gesuita tedesco Johann Adam Schall von Bell.

Южный католический собор（俄文）

Находится на северо-востоке от ворот Сюаньумэнь. Был построен в 1605 г. итальянским миссионером Маттео Риччи (китайское имя － Ли Мадоу) и немецким миссионером Тан Жован.

천주교 남당（韩文）

쉬안우문(宣武門) 동북쪽에 위치해 있으며 명나라 만력 33년(1605년)에 선후하여 이탈리아 전도사 이마두(마테오 리치)와 독일 전교사 아담 샬 폰 벨에 의하여 수건되었다.

什刹海

元代称为"海子",是南北大运河漕运的终点,曾经十分繁荣。明清以来,这里修建了许多王公贵族的园林别墅和寺庙。如今,什刹海沿岸酒吧密布,成为集自然景观,人文历史,市井文化于一身的旅游胜地。

Shichahai Lake (英文)

Named Haizi in the Yuan Dynasty, the lake is the northern terminal of the Grand Canal. During the Ming and Qing dynasties, villas of princes and aristocrats, as well as Buddhist temples, were erected here. Nowadays, the lake is surrounded by countless bars and restaurants, forming a tourist attraction integrating natural scenery, culture and folk customs.

什刹海 (日文)

元の時は「海子」と呼ばれ、南北大運河の北の終着地として、かつては大変な繁栄を見せた。明・清いらい、あたりには多くの王族の邸宅や別荘、庭園と仏寺が建てられた。今日の什刹海はバーが密集し、自然景色、人文歴史、市井文化を一体に集めた観光の勝地となっている。

Lago Shichahai (西文)

En los años de la dinastía Yuan, fue este el animado puerto extremo del Gran Canal. A partir de las dinastías Ming y Qing, se levantaron aquí las mansiones y jardines de los nobles y los templos. Actualmente, alrededor del lago se concentran muchos bares que hacen del lugar un sitio muy concurrido.

Shichahai (德文)

Es handelt sich dabei um die drei Seen Xihai, Houhai und Qianhai im Westen des Di'anmen-Tors des Stadtbezirkes Xicheng. Früher bidelte Shichahai das nördliche Ende des Großen Kanals. Während der Ming- und Qing-Dynastie entstanden hier viele kaiserliche Gartenanlagen und Residenzen der hohen Beamten. Heute zieht diese Gegend mit zahlreichen Bars viele in- und ausländische Touristen an.

Lo Shichahai (意大利文)

All'epoca della dinastia Yuan era chiamato "Haizi", quando era un porto e un florido centro di trasporto di cereali. A partire dalle dinastie Ming e Qing, i principi e i nobili scelsero quest'area per edificarvi le proprie residenze e numerosi templi. Oggi lungo il lago Shichahai sono presenti numerosi localini e ristoranti che costituiscono un'area ricreativa molto amata dai giovani locali e dai turisti, in cui il paesaggio del lago, la storia e la cultura si combinano armoniosamente.

Озеро Шицахай (俄文)

В династии Юань называется «Хайцзы». Тогда берег озера был портом для транспортировки продовольствия. Было шумно и многолюдно. Во время династии Мин и Цин на берегах озера были сооружены многие сады, храмы и резиденции чиновников и аристократов. В настоящее время по берегам озера протянутся много баров.

스차하이 (韩文)

스차하이(십찰해)는 원나라 시기에는 "해자(海子)"라고 불렸고 남북 대운하의 종점이였으며 당시에는 아주 번화하였다. 명·청나라 이후 줄곧 여러 왕궁귀족의 별장과 사찰을 수건하였다. 현재 스차하이 주변은 술집이 밀집되고 자연풍경, 인문역사, 통속문화를 한몸에 지닌 유람성지로 되었다.

Le lac des Dix Monastères (法文)

Le lac des Dix Monastères (Shichahai), appelé "Haizi" sous les Yuan, était le point final du Grand Canal, où régnait autrefois une extrême animation. Depuis les Ming et les Qing, on a construit autour de ce lac de nombreux jardins, résidences et temples pour des princes et des nobles. Aujourd'hui, le lac Shichahai, bordé de bars serrés, est devenu un lieu touristique réputé pour ses beaux paysages naturels, son histoire ancienne et sa culture traditionnelle.

王府井大街

明朝永乐年间（1417年）在这一带修建了十座王府，称为王府街、后因有著名的水井，称为王府井大街，清末王府井大街成为著名的商业街。现在的王府井大街成为北京最繁华的商业街之一。

Wangfujing Street （英文）

In 1417 during the Yongle reign period of the Ming Dynasty, this street contained ten wangfu (princes' mansions), and was thus called Wangfu Street. At its north end is a well (*jing*), and the street was later renamed Wangfujing Street. In the late Qing Dynasty, it developed into a famous commercial street. It is still one of the busiest commercial streets in Beijing.

王府井大街 （日文）

明の永楽年間(1417年)は、10の王府(皇族の邸宅)があることから「王府街」と称されたが、後に井戸も掘られたため、王府井大街に名が改められた。清末からの名高いビジネス街で、現在は北京一をほこる繁華街である。

왕푸징(王府井)거리 （韩文）

명나라 영락년간(1417년)에 여기에 10개의 왕부를 수건하여 이곳을 왕부거리라고 불렸는데 후에는 유명한 우물 때문에 이곳을 왕푸징거리라고 불렀으며 청나라 말년에는 이곳은 유명한 상업거리로 소문났다. 지금의 왕푸징거리는 베이징에서 가장 번화한 상업거리 중의 하나이다.

La via Wangfujing （意大利文）

Durante il periodo del regno dell'imperatore Yongle della dinastia Ming, qui furono edificate dieci residenze imperiali, da cui deriva il nome Wangfu (appunto, residenze imperiali). E poiché in seguito vi fu scavato anche un pozzo famoso il nome della via assunse quello conosciuto fino ad oggi, di Wangfujing (il pozzo delle residenze imperiali). Alla fine della dinastia Qing la Wangfujing divenne una via commerciale molto fiorente, proprio come lo è ancora oggi, sebbene diversa e moderna rispetto al passato.

Пешеходный проспект Ванфуцзинь (俄文)

В 1417 году были построены 10 княжеских дворцов. Тогда этот проспект назывался Ванфуцзе. Потом из известного колодца переименовался в Ванфуцзинь. В конце династии Цин Ванфуце стал известным коммерческим проспектом. Нынешний Ванфуцзинь – один из самых шумных проспектов в Пекине.

La rue de Wangfujing （法文）

Sous le règne Yongle (1417) de l'empereur Chengzu des Ming, une dizaine de résidences princières furent construites à cet endroit, ce qui lui a valu le nom de la rue Wangfu (résidences princières). Plus tard, un puits creusé sur l'emplacement était connu de tout le monde et cette rue a reçu son nom actuel (Wangfujing, Puits des résidences princières). A la fin des Qing, cette rue est devenue un quartier commercial célèbre. Aujourd'hui, la rue de Wangfujing est l'une des rues commerçantes les plus animées de Beijing.

Wangfujing （德文）

Wangfujing ist die lebhafteste Geschäftsstraße Beijings. Im Jahre 1417 während der Yongle-Regierungsperiode der Ming-Dynastie wurden hier zehn Prinzenresidenzen errichtet. Da hier damals einen Brunnen gab, erhielt sie den heutigen Namen. Schon Ende der Qing-Dynastie war Wangfujing als eine Geschäftsstraße bekannt.

Calle Wangfujing （西文）

En 1417 se construyeron en esta zona las mansiones de diez príncipes. Wangfujing significa el pozo de las mansiones de príncipes. En los últimos años de la dinastía Qing, la calle se había convertido en un famoso centro comercial de la ciudad y actualmente sigue siendo la calle más próspera de Beijing.

新东安市场

东安市场是北京建立最早的一座综合市场，已有100多年历史，1998年东安市场在新东安商厦内重新开张。

Sun Dong'an Market （英文）

The predecessor of the Sun Dong'an Market, Dong'an Market, was one of the oldest comprehensive shopping venues in Beijing. In 1998, it was reopened as the newly renovated Sun Dong'an Market.

新東安市場 （日文）

新東安市場。北京最古の総合的なマーケットである。すでに100年あまりの歴史がある。現在の建物は1998年、東安市場跡地に新たに建てられたものである。

신둥안(新東安)시장 （韩文）

신둥안(新東安) 시장, 둥안(東安) 시장은 베이징에서 건립된 최초의 종합시장으로 이미 100 여년의 역사를 가지고 있으며 1998 년에 둥안시장은 신둥안빌딩에서 새로 오픈하였다.

Le nouveau marché Dong'an （法文）

Le marché Dong'an est le premier grand marché ouvert à Beijing, ayant déjà plus de 100 ans d'histoire. En 1998, ce marché a été ouvert à nouveau dans son nouveau bâtiment.

Das Warenhaus Xindong'an （德文）

Das Warenhaus Xindong'an liegt an der Geschäftsstraße Wangfujing und wurde im Jahre 1998 an der Stelle des hundertjährigen Warenhauses Dong'an errichtet.

Plaza Sun Dong'an （意大利文）

Il mercato Dong'an fu il primo grande magazzino costruito a Pechino, ha una storia di oltre 100 anni. Nel 1988, il mercato Dong'an è stato riaperto nel Sun Dong'an Plaza.

Дунъань Шичан （俄文）

Рынок Дунъань Шичан был самым древним рынком в Пекине. Он имеет почти 100-летнюю историю. В 1998 году этот рынок был перестроен в универмаг «Синьдунъань Шичан».

Nueva Plaza Dong´an （西文）

Nueva Plaza Dong´an, reabierta en 1998. Su predecesora fue el Mercado Dong´an, el más antiguo de Beijing, con más de cien años de historia.

大栅栏

明、清两代，北京入夜常实行"宵禁"，街头巷尾处处设置栅栏，是为大栅栏名称的由来。这条全长270米的小街中集中了很多有名的老字号商铺，成为老北京传统商业文化特色的典型。

Dashilan（英文）

During the Ming and Qing dynasties, a curfew was frequently imposed at night. Barriers (pronounced by locals as *shilan*) were erected at both ends of streets and alleys. The 270-meter-long street contains many traditional shops, making it a typical commercial street of old Beijing.

大柵欄（日文）

長さ270mで、老舗が建ち並んだ北京市の伝統商業文化の町である。明・清両代の北京は、夜になると街のあちこちに柵欄(やらい)を設けて夜間取り締まりをしたことがしばしばある。大柵欄という呼び名はこれにちなんだものである。

Улица Дачжалань（барьер）（俄文）

Во время династии Мин и Цин ночью в Пекине часто объявился комендантский час. В городе повсюду были установлены барьеры. Из этого взялось название улицы. На 270-метровой улицы сосредоточены много известных старых магазинов. Дачжалань уже стал образцом традиционной коммерческой культуры старого Пекина.

Dashilan （德文）

Dashilan ist eine berühmte Geschäftsstraße Bejings. Sie liegt im Süden des Qianmen-Tors. Obwohl sie nur 270 m lang und 4 bis 7 m breit ist, bildet sie mit zahlreichen alten Gschäften und Theatern das Zentrum des ältesten Geschäftsviertels Beijings. Früher hieß sie die 4. Langfang-Straße. Seit der Mitte der Qing-Dynastie trägt sie den heutigen Namen, weil damals an ihren beiden Eingängen zwei große Gittertore errichtet wurden.

Calle Dashilan（西文）

Durante las dinastías Ming y Qing se impuso el toque de queda por la noche y por eso se colocaron barreras en cada bocacalle de la zona urbana. Dashilan en chino, significa justamente barrera. Los centenares de tiendas famosas que se encuentran en esta calle de 270 m. de largo la convirtieron en la arteria comercial más representativa de Beijing.

L'area di Dashilan（意大利文）

Durante le dinastia Ming e Qing, Pechino veniva chiusa la notte nelle ore di coprifuoco per cui la parte iniziale e finale della via venivano serrate; da questa tradizione deriva il nome della via di Dashilan. In origine, lungo la via Dashilan, lunga 270 metri, si trovano antiche botteghe che rappresentano la tradizione culturale e commerciale dell'antica Pechino.

Dashilan （法文）

Sous les Ming et les Qing, les autorités décrétaient souvent le couvre-feu en mettant des barrières dans les rues, ce qui aurait donné l'origine à son nom. Le long de cette petite rue de 270 mètres de long sont réunies un grand nombre de vieilles boutiques célèbres, ce qui l'a rendue renommée pour son commerce et sa culture traditionnelle.

다짜란(大柵欄)（韩文）

다짜란은 중국말로 울타리란 뜻이다. 명·청 두 나라시기 베이징은 밤에 늘 "통행금지"를 시켯기 때문에 거리마다 울타리를 둘렀다. 이것이 다짜란 이름 유래이다. 총 길이가 270m인 작은 거리에 많은 유명한 노포들이 줄지어 있는데 노 베이징 전통 상업문화를 반영한 전형이다.

琉璃厂

元、明两代，这里是烧制琉璃瓦的官窑。清代，这里聚集了各地的会馆，逐渐成为书籍、古玩书画、笔墨纸砚的经营街。

Liulichang（英文）

A government kiln stood here producing glazed tiles during the Yuan and Ming dynasties. Many guild halls were located here during the Qing Dynasty, and it later developed into a street selling old books, antiques, calligraphy, painting, brushes, ink and ink stones.

琉璃廠（日文）

元・明両代は皇室用の瑠璃かわらを焼く窯が設けられたところで、清代からは会館が多く設立され、だんだん今日のように古書、骨董および「文房四宝」と呼ばれる筆墨紙硯を専門的に扱う町となった。

Calle Liulichang（西文）

A partir de las dinastías Yuan y Ming, esta vía se dedicó a la fabricación de las tejas vidriadas. En los años de la dinastía Qing se transformó poco a poco en un centro comercial de utensilios de escritorio.

Liulichang（法文）

Sous les Ming et les Qing, la rue de Liulichang était occupée par un four impérial pour cuire des tuiles vernissées. Sous les Qing, les foyers des associations de compatriotes de diverses régions s'y installèrent et peu à peu, s'est formée une rue spécialisée dans la vente des livres, des antiquités, des calligraphies, des peintures et des fournitures de bureau comme le pinceau, le papier, l'encre et l'encrier.

Liulichang （德文）

Liulichang ist eine berühmte Kunst- und Antiquitätenstraße in der Nähe des Hepingmen-Tors des Stadtbezirkes Xuanwu. In der Ming- und Qing-Dynastie gab es hier Werkstätten für glasierte Ziegel, die für den Bau der kaiserlichen Paläste bestimmt waren. Heute gibt es hier vielle Läden, wo Antiquitäten, Malereien, kalligrafische Werke, kunsthandwerkliche Produkte und auch die „vier Schätze der Studierstube" — Papier, Pinsel, Tusche und Tuschstein — angeboten werden.

Il *Liulichang* （意大利文）

Durante le dinastie Yuan e Ming, sulla via Liulichang si trovavano le fornaci imperiali per la produzione di tegole e delle mattonelle in ceramica. Dalla fine della dinastia Ming, presso poco a poco a stabilirvisi anche rivenditori di libri, calligrafi, produttori di stampe e rilegatori. Nacquero così laboratori per la stampa e piccoli negozi, dove i letterati potevano trovare tutto quanto servivano loro per praticare l'arte della calligrafia: calamai in pietra, pennelli, carta e timbri. Ancora oggi visitare Liulichang è un'esperienza molto speciale.

Улица Люличан（俄文）

Во время династии Юань и Мин на этой улочке обосновались мастера по обжигу глазурованной черепицы, предназначенной для императорского дворца. В династии Цин здесь появился первый самый большой книжный рынок в Пекине. Потом на Люличан в основном продавались древние книги, свитки, антиквариат, образцы каллиграфии, ювелирные изделия, произведения резчиков по камню, нефриту и т. д.

류리창(琉璃場)（韩文）

원·명두나라 시기 전문 유리기와를 만드는 관청의 가마공장이였다. 청나라 때 여러 지역의 회관이 집중되어 점차적으로 서류, 골동품, 종이, 붓 등을 경영하는 거리로 되었다.

北京烤鸭

　　北京烤鸭有全聚德的挂炉和便宜坊的焖炉两种，都是京城老字号。

　　北京ダックの丸焼き「北京烤鸭」。老舗・全聚徳の「掛け炉ダック」と便宜坊の「火蒸ダック」の2種類のものがある。

　　베이징 오리구이는 취안쥐더(全聚德)의 불위에 걸어 굽는 방법과 펜이팡(便宜坊)의 화덕에 넣고 굽는 방법 두 가지가 있는데 모두 베이징의 노포이다.

　　Beijing roast duck comes in two categories: Gualu Roast Duck (duck roasted over a fire) which the Quanjude restaurants specialize in, and Menlu Roast Duck (duck roasted in an oven) which the Bianyifang restaurants specialize in. Both Quanjude and Bianyifang are time-honored roast duck restaurants in Beijing.

涮羊肉

　　涮羊肉是北京冬令佳肴，最有名的是老字号东来顺饭庄。

　　Mongolian hotpot is a winter cuisine of local flavor, and the most famous hotpot provider in Beijing is the time-honored Donglaishun Restaurant.

Le canard laqué de Beijing est préparé selon deux méthodes de rôtissage différentes : le four ouvert aux crochets du restaurant Quanjude (Réunion de toutes les vertus) et le four fermé du restaurant Bianyifang (Au bon marché). Tous les deux sont les vieux restaurants de Beijing, réputés pour le canard laqué de leur propre marque.

Peking-Ente ist ein berühmtes Gericht der chinesischen Küche. In den Restaurants Quanjude und Bianyifang kann man die typische Peking-Ente probieren.

Пекинскую утку можно кушать в ресторанах Цюаньцзюйдэ и Бяньифан, которые являются старыми ресторанами в Пекине.

"Anatra laccata" pechinese. Esistono due scuole di preparazione della Kaoya (letteralmente oca arrosto). Una di esse fa uso del forno a legna senza chiusura in cui si bruciano legni che non emettono fumo come quello di giuggiolo, di pesco e di pero profumati e adatti per far assumere un gusto fruttato alla pelle croccante dell'oca. L'altra scuola fa invece uso di un comune forno a legna in cui il fuoco non arde a contatto diretto con l'oca, ma la si cuoce con il calore delle braci accese.

Pato Laqueado, alimento famoso y tradicional de Beijing. Puede prepararse de dos formas, como muestran los restaurantes Quanjude y Bianyifang.

北京の冬の名物－羊のしゃぶしゃぶ。東来順はその老舗で北京でもっとも有名。

양고기 샤브샤브는 베이징 겨울음식 중의 별미로 가장 유명한 것은 노포 둥라이순관점(東來順飯莊)의 것이다.

La marmite mongole (fondue) est un plat d'hiver exquis à Beijing. La plus connue est celle du vieux restaurant Donglaishun.

Hammelfleisch-Feuertopf ist in Beijing ein Lieblingsgericht im Winter. Donglaishun ist das berühmste Restaurant für solches Gericht.

La "Pentola Mongola" è un piatto speciale invernale molto amato dai pechinesi. Il Ristorante Donglaishun è il più rinomato a Pechino del suo genere.

Шуаньянжоу, баранина, сваренная в китайском самоваре – это одно из популярных блюд в зимнем Пекине. Самый известный ресторан, где подают шуаньянжоу, — это старый ресторан «Дунлайшунь».

La Olla Mongola es un plato muy demandado, sobre todo en el invierno. Se considera el de mejor sabor el preparado por el restaurante Donglaishun.

长安大戏院

长安大戏院始建于1937年的老字号剧场，原址在西单路口，新建的长安大戏院以上演经典京剧剧目为主。

The Chang'an Grand Theater, first built in 1937, was originally located at the entrance to Xidan Street. The new Chang'an Grand Theater is mainly used to stage classical Peking opera.

長安大戲院。1937年に建設がはじまった芝居舞台の「老舗」。もともとは西単の四つ辻にあったが、現在のものは場所を変えて新築したもので、京劇の経典演目の公演を主としている。

창안대극원은 1937년에 역사를 가진 노극장으로 원래는 시단(西單)길 어구에 있었으며 새로 건축한 창안대극원은 유명한 경극절목만 연출하고 있다.

L'ancien Grand Théâtre Chang'an, construit en 1937, était au carrefour de Xidan. Le Grand Théâtre Chang'an nouvellement construit a principalement pour mission de monter des pièces classiques d'Opéra de Beijing.

Das Theater Chang'an wurde im Jahre 1937 mit dem Sitz in Xidan gebaut und gehört zu den ältesten Theatern Beijings. Das neue Theater liegt an der Straße Jianguomenwai-Straße. Hier werden haupsächlich die klassischen Stücke der Peking-Oper aufgeführt.

Il Teatro Chang'an fu costruito nel 1937 all'inizio della via Xidan su cui fu poi ricostruito il nuovo Teatro Chang'an, dove le opere rappresentate sono principalmente dell'Opera di Pechino.

Чанъаньский театр был построен в 1937 году, тогда он находился на улице Сидань. Теперь в театре главным образом идут спектакля пекинской оперы.

Cuando abrió sus puertas, en 1937, el Teatro Chang'an se situaba en la bocacalle de Xidan. Su sede actual se dedica principalmente a los espectáculos de la Ópera de Pekín.

京剧

京剧已有200多年历史。京剧的唱腔、脸谱、服饰、表演，包括经典剧目，以及诸流派和著名的表演艺术家，都使京剧成为真实的国家艺术瑰宝。

Peking opera has a history of more than 200 years. As a national artistic treasure, it is renowned for its distinctive melodies, facial makeup, costumes and acting techniques, as well as a number of prestigious performers in different genres.

中国の京劇はすでに200年以上の歴史がある。独特な歌、くま取り、服飾と演技があり、経典演目や流派と名高い俳優も多い。京劇は中国を代表する国の宝である。

경극은 이미 200년의 역사를 가지고 있다. 경극의 노래곡조, 분장, 복장, 표현 및 명대목, 여러 파벌의 저명한 경극표현가 등 여러 가지 인소들은 경극을 중국예술의 진귀한 보물로 부상시켰다.

L'Opéra de Beijing a déjà plus de 200 ans d'histoire. De par ses chants mélodieux, ses personnages aux visages peints fort variés et aux costumes splendides, son jeu de scène captivant, son riche répertoire classique, ses écoles de différents styles et ses nombreux fameux acteurs, l'Opéra de Beijing est devenu le véritable trésor artistique de Chine.

Die Peking-Oper hat eine Geschichte von mehr als 200 Jahren. Bei dieser Operat sind Gesang, Rezitation, Pantomien und Akrobatik miteinander verbunden.

L'Opera di Pechino vanta una storia di oltre 200 anni. La parte vocale, le maschere, i costumi, le opere e gli artisti costituiscono nel loro insieme un importante tesoro nazionale dell'arte nazionale.

Пекинская опера имеет почти 200-летнюю историю. Это комплексный вид искусства, включающий в себя пение, танец, речитативы и акробатику. Пение, густой грим на лицах, костюмы, классические спектакля и выдающие актеры сделали эту оперу жемчужиной искусства.

La Ópera de Pekín, con más de 200 años de historia, es considerada un tesoro artístico nacional por sus melodías, cantos, máscaras, vestimentas, obras, variedad de sectas y famosos actores.

同仁堂

同仁堂老字号药店开业于1669年，以优质中草药和各种中药成药闻名于世。

Tongrentang Pharmacy, established in 1669, is famous for high-quality medical herbs and traditional Chinese medications.

１６６９年開業の漢方薬の老舗－同仁堂。品質が高く効き目が抜群の漢方既製薬の提供で名が広く世界に知れ渡っている。

동인당(同仁堂) 약국은 1669년 개업한 노포로 양호한 품질의 중초약과 각 종 중약으로 유명하다.

La vieille pharmacie Tongrentang, créée en 1669, est réputée pour ses herbes médicinales et ses drogues de qualité.

Die Apotheke Tongrentang befindet sich der Dashilan-Straße. Sie wurde im Jahre 1669 errichtet und ist wegen ihrer ausgezeichneten traditionellen chinesischen Arznei nicht nur im Inland, sondern auch im Ausland bekannt.

La farmacia Tongrentang fu avviata nel 1669, nota in tutto il mondo per le sue medicine di erbe officinali-medicinali tipiche della medicina tradizionale cinese.

Старая аптека «Тунжэньтан» открылась в 1669 году. Она известна всему миру своими качественными китайскими лекарственными растениями и готовыми лекарствами китайской медицины.

La farmacia Tongrentang se inauguró en 1669 y se hizo famosa por sus medicamentos de calidad, elaborados según los métodos de la medicina tradicional china.

仿膳饭庄

仿膳饭庄开业于1925年，其菜肴糕点都按清朝御膳房的标准制作。地址设在北海公园琼华岛北侧的古建筑群中。

Fangshan Restaurant, established in 1925, huddles among ancient buildings in the north of Jade Islet in Beihai Park. It specializes in Qing Dynasty imperial cuisine.

１９２５年開業の仿膳飯荘飯。すべての料理やスナックは清代の御膳房の標準にしたがって調理する。北海公園瓊華島北側の古代建築群の中にある。

광산판점(仿膳饭庄)은 1925년에 개업하였으며 음식과 후식은 모두 청나라의 어선방의 표준으로 제작한다. 지점은 베이하이공원 충다오섬 북쪽의 고대 건축물군 속에 있다.

Le restaurant Fangshan (A l'imitation de la cuisine impériale) fut ouvert en 1925. Ses mets et ses gâteaux sont tous préparés selon la spécification de qualité de la cuisine de la cour des Qing. Ce restaurant est dans un ensemble architectural de la partie nord de l'île Qionghua dans le Parc Beihai.

Das Restaurant Fangshan befindet sich im Beihai-Park und wurde im Jahre 1925 gebaut. Hier kann die Gerichte der kaiserlichen Küche probieren.

Il ristorante Fangshan fu aperto nel 1925. I suoi piatti e i suoi dolci vengono preparati secondo la tradizione dalla cucina imperiale della dinastia Qing. Il ristorante si trova a nord dell'Isola del Fiore di Giada nel parco Beihai.

Ресторан «Фаншань» открылся в 1925 году. Блюда и десерты готовятся по рецептам цинской императорской кухни. Ресторан находится в древнем ансамбле на севере острова Цюнхуадао парка Бэйхай.

En la isla Qiongdao, del Palacio de Invierno, se abrió en 1925 el restaurante Fangshan, cuyos platillos se preparan según los métodos de la cocina imperial de la dinastía Qing.

文天祥祠

文天祥为南宋民族英雄，曾率兵抗击元军，兵败被俘，英勇就义。

Wen Tianxiang of the Southern Song Dynasty was a hero of the resistance to the Mongol invaders.

文天祥氏は南宋時代の民族英雄である。兵を率いて元軍に反撃した時、不幸にも逮捕されて英雄的な死を遂げた。

문천상은 남송의 민족영웅이고 병사를 이끌고 원(몽골)군과 저항하다가 패하여 포로되었으며 죽을 때까지 투항하지않은 민족영웅이다.

Wen Tianxian, héros national des Song du Sud, commanda ses soldats pour résister aux troupes des Yuan. Capturé par l'ennemi, il mourut en héros.

Der Tempel für Wen Tianxiang liegt an der Xuefu-Straße des Stadtbezirkes Dongcheng und wurde im Jahre 1376 für Wen Tianxiang, einen bekannten General der Südlichen Song-Dynastie gebaut.

Questo tempio fu edificato per commemorare Wen Tianxiang, eroe nazionale della dinastia Song Meridionale, che fu arrestato ed ucciso dai nemici dopo la sconfitta della battaglia contro le truppe Yuan.

Вэнь Тяньсян – национальный герой в династии Наньсун. Он погиб в борьбе с монгольскими завоевателями.

Wen Tianxiang, famoso héroe de la nación Han, de la dinastía Song del Sur, dirigió las tropas ante la invasión de los mongoles. Después de ser capturado por éstos, se negó a rendirse y fue ejecutado.

曹雪芹纪念馆

中国古典文学巨著《红楼梦》的作者曹雪芹晚年在西山生活和写作。纪念馆即他当年的故居。

Cao Xueqin, author of the classic *A Dream of Red Mansions*, lived in Xishan during his late years. The memorial hall was built on the basis of his former residence there.

中国古典文学の大作『紅楼夢』の作者・曹雪芹氏が晩年西山に暮らして創作に没頭した。記念館は氏が住んでいたところ。

중국고전문학의 저작《홍루몽》의 작가 차오쉐친은 만년에 서산에서 생활하고 습작하였다. 기념관은 그가 당년에 살던 집이다.

Cao Xueqin, auteur du roman classique *Le Rêve dans le Pavillon rouge*, ouvrage monumental dans l'histoire de la littérature chinoise, vivait et écrivait pendant ses dernières années au pied des Collines de l'Ouest. Le présent mémorial était son ancienne demeure.

Die Gedenknalie für Cao Xueqin befindet sich in der Nähe des Biyun-Tempels des Stadtbezirkes Haidian. Cao Xueqin, Autor des berühmten klassischen Romans „Der Traum der Roten Kammer", verbracht hier seinen Lebensabend.

Questo edificio fu la residenza dello scrittore Cao Xueqin, autore del classico "Sogno della Camara Rossa". Qui visse fino alla sua morte.

Здесь жил и занимался творчеством Цао Сюецинь, писатель «Сон в красном тереме» в последние годы жизни.

Cao Xueqin, gran escritor y autor de la obra maestra "El Sueño de la Mansión Roja", pasó su vejez en esta casa ubicada en las montañas occidentales de Beijing.

宋庆龄故居

宋庆龄故居位于后海北岸，原为清朝的王府花园，宋庆龄1963年迁居于此，直到逝世。

The Former Residence of Soong Ching-ling, on the north bank of Houhai Lake, was an imperial garden during the Qing Dynasty. She retired here in 1963.

後海の北岸にある。清代の王府花園にあたったところ。宋慶齢氏は1963年からここに移って、この世を去るまで住んでいた。

쑹칭링고택은 허우하이 북안에 위치해 있으며 원래 청나라의 왕부정원이었다. 쑹칭링은 1963년에 이곳에 이사했으며 별세할 때까지 이곳에서 살았다.

L'ancienne résidence de Soong Ching-ling est située sur la rive nord du lac de Derrière. C'était à l'origine le jardin d'un prince. En 1963, Soong Ching-ling déménagea à cet endroit et y vécut jusqu'à la fin de sa vie.

Dre Wohnstätte Soong Ching-lings liegt am Nordufer des Houhai-Sees des Staqdtbezirkes Xicheng. In der Qing-Zeit gehörte sie zum Garten einer Prinzenresidenz. Von 1963 an verbracht Soong Ching-ling, die Witwe von Dr. Sun Yat-see, hier ihren Lebensabend.

Situata sulla riva settentrionale del lago Houhai, in origine questa residenza era un giardino imperiale della dinastia Qing. Soong Qing Ling vi abitò dal 1963 fino alla sua scomparsa.

Находится на северном берегу озера Хоухай. Сначала это был садом цинского дворца. В 1963 году Сун Цинлин переселилась туда. Здесь она провела последние годы жизни.

La mansión se sitúa en la orilla norteña del lago Houhai y originalmente perteneció al príncipe . A partir de 1963 Soong Ching Ling, viuda del Dr. Sun Yatsen, se mudó a élla y vivió allí hasta su muerte.

北京商务中心区、位于朝阳区、东长安街两侧，规划面积近 4 平方公里。

The Central Business District of Beijing occupies nearly four square kilometers along East Chang'an Avenue in Chaoyang District.

北京商務中心区（ＣＢＤ）。市の朝陽区と東長安街両側をカバーしており、計画総面積は 4 ㎞² に近い。

베이징상업중심구는 차오양구에 위치하여 있는데 둥창안가의 양쪽에 위치해 있으며 면적은 거의 4 ㎢에 달한다.

La Zone centrale des affaires de Beijing (CBD), située des deux côtés de l'Avenue Chang'an de l'Est dans l'arrondissement de Chaoyang, occupe 4 kilomètres carrés selon le projet.

Das Businesscentre Beijings liegt an der beiden Seiten der östlichen Chang'an-Straße des Stadtbezirkes Chaoyang. Die geplante Fläche erreicht 4 Quadratmeter.

La Zona centrale commerciale di Beijing si trova nel distretto di Chaoyang, ai due lati della via Chang'an (della Lunga Pace). L'area comprende una superficie di quattro chilometri quadrati.

Пекинская центральная деловая часть в районе Чаоян находится на обеих сторонах проспекта Дунчанъанцзе. Планированная площадь части составляет 4 кв. км.

CBD (Distrito Central de Negocios, siglas en inglés) de Beijing, ubicado a ambos lados de la Avenida Chang'an del Este, en el distrito de Chaoyang, sobre una superficie planificada de casi 4 km².

燕莎友谊商城，是中国第一家开业的中外合资、现代化高档零售商场。

Lufthansa Friendship Shopping City was the first joint-venture shopping mall in contemporary China.

燕莎友誼商城(ルフトハンザ・マーケット)。中国最初の現代化された中外合資の高級小売マーケット。

옌사유이상점는 중국 최초로 개발된 중외합작의 현대화 고급 상가이다.

Le Centre commercial d'amitié de Lufthansa est le premier grand magasin de détail haut de gamme aux capitaux mixtes, ouvert en Chine.

Lufthansa Centre ist das erste chinesisch-ausländische Gemeinschaftsunternehmen Chinas. Hier werden teure Qualitätswaren angeboten.

Il centro commerciale Lufthansa fu il primo centro commerciale a capitale cinese e straniero insieme aperto in Cina negli anni '90.

Универмаг «Яньша» — первый совместный универмаг с иностранными инвестициями в Китае.

Centro Comercial de Lufthansa, primer espacio de su tipo abierto en Beijing con capital mixto para las compras de alta categoría.

中国大饭店
China World Hotel
ホテルの中国大飯店
중국대판점
Hôtel mondial de Chine

China World Hotel
Hotel China World
Гостиница «Чжунго Дафаньдянь»
Hotel Mundial de China

京广中心
Jingguang Center
京広センター
징광센터
Le Centre Beijing-Guangzhou

Jingguang Centre Hotel
Jing Guang New World Hotel
Гостиница Цзингуан Чжунсинь
Edificio del Centro Jingguang

长城饭店
Beijing Great Wall Sheraton Hotel
ホテルの長城飯店
창청호텔
Hôtel de la Grande Muraille
Great Wall Sheraton Hotel
L'hotel Sheraton Grande Muraglia
Гостиница «Чанчэнь»
Hotel Gran Muralla

复兴门金融街
Financial Street
復興門の金融街
베이징 금융가
La rue de la Finance de Beijing
Die Finanzstraße Beijings
La Via finanziaria di Pechino
Улица Цзиньжунцзе
Calle financiera de Beijing

金融街街标
The symbol of the Financial Street
金融街ランドマーク
금융가 표시
Emblème de la rue de la Finance
Kennzeichen der Finanzstraße
Il simbolo della Via finanziaria
Знак улицы Цзиньжунцзе
Emblema de la calle financiera

东方广场位于王府井商业街南口，占地10万平方米，集商业、购物、休闲、娱乐、办公于一体，是亚洲最大的商业建筑群。

Standing by the south entrance to the Wangfujing Street, Oriental Plaza covers 10 hectares, and combines commerce, shopping, recreation, entertainment and office buildings. It is said to be the largest commercial complex in Asia.

王府井ビジネス街にある東方広場。敷地面積は10万m²。ビジネス、ショッピング、レジャー、レクリエーション、オフィスビルを一体に集めた建築群である。

동팡광장은 왕푸징상업거리의 남쪽에 위치하여 있으며 면적은 10 만㎡이고 상업, 쇼핑, 레저, 오락, 비지니스를 일체로 하는 아세아 최대 상업 건축군이다.

Situé à l'extrémité sud de la rue de Wangfujing, l'Oriental Plaza (Place de l'Orient) occupe 100 000 mètres carrés de surface. Combinant les fonctions de commerce, d'achat, de repos, de distraction et de travail dans un bureau, il représente le plus vaste ensemble d'architecture commerciale en Asie.

Oriental Plaza liegt am südlichen Eingang der Geschäftsstraße Wangfujing und ist mit einer Fläche von 100 000 Quadratmetern der größte Gebäudekomplex Asiens.

L'Oriental Plaza si trova nella parte meridionale della via commerciale Wangfujing, e ricopre una superficie di 100.000 metri quadrati. È uno dei complessi commerciali fra i più grandi dell'Asia e comprende ogni tipo di attività commerciale, fra cui negozi delle più note firme internazionali, shopping, cinema, librerie, cafetterie, ristoranti di ogni tipo ed anche uffici.

Торговый центр «Дунфан Гуанчан» находится на юге улицы Ванфуцзин, Общая площадь составляет 100 тыс. кв. м. Дунфан Гуанчан является крупнейшим коммерческим ансамблем в Азии.

Plaza del Oriente, en el sur de la calle Wangfujing. Ocupa una superficie de 100.000 metros cuadrados. Es el mayor conjunto comercial de Asia, en el cual se concentran centros comerciales y recreativos y oficinas.

中国美术馆，是一座展示、收藏、研究中国近现代艺术作品的国家级美术馆。

The National Art Museum of China is used for exhibition and collection of and research into contemporary Chinese arts.

中国美術館。中国近・現代芸術作品の展示、収蔵と研究を専門とする国家クラス美術館である。

중국미술관은 중국 근・현대예술작품을 전시, 수집, 연구하는 국가급 미술관이다.

Le Palais des Beaux-Arts de Chine est spécialisé dans l'exposition, la collection et l'étude des œuvres d'art modernes chinoises.

Museo de Bellas Artes de China, dedicado a la exhibición, colección y estudio de las obras modernas.

Die Kunstgalerie Chinas, an der nördlichen Seite der Dongsi-Straße des Stadtbezirkes Dongcheng gelegen, ist das Zentrum für die Sammlung und das Studium der Kunstwerke aus der Vergangenheit und der Gegenwart Chinas.

Il Museo di Belle Arti cinesi è un museo di livello nazionale in cui, oltre alle mostre presentate regolarmente, si portano avanti studi di restauro e ricerca delle opere moderne cinesi.

Китайский художественный музей является государственным музеем, где выставляются, хранятся и изучаются китайские новые и современные художественные произведения.

首都博物馆新馆　首都博物館新館 수도박물관신관
The newly built Capital Museum
Le nouveau bâtiment du Musée de la Capitale
Das neue Shoudu-Museum
Il nuovo Edificio del Museo della Capitale
Новый павильон столичного музея
Nuevo Museo de la Capital

西单图书大厦，是北京规模最大的图书销售和物流中心。
The Xidan Book Building is the largest book sale and distribution center in Beijing.
西单図書大厦ビル。北京では最大規模の図書の販売と交流センターである。
시단도서빌딩은 베이징 최대 규모의 도서판매 물류중심이다.
Le Bâtiment du Livre de Xidan est le plus grand centre de vente et de distribution des livres de Beijing
Das Bücher-Gebäude in Xidan ist die größte Buchhandlung Beijings.
Quella di Xidan è la libreria più grande a Pechino
Книжное здание «Сидань» является крупнейшим в Пекине центром продажи и материально-технического обеспечения книг
Plaza de Libros de Xidan, el mayor centro de venta y logística de libros en Beijing.

北京音乐厅.
The Beijing Concert Hall
北京音楽ホール
베이징음악청
La Salle de concert de Beijing
Die Musikhalle Beijings
Пекинский концертный зал
Salón de Conciertos de Beijing
La Sale di Concerto di Beijing

91

中华民族园是国内最大的展示各民族传统建筑，民俗风情、歌舞表演、工艺制作和美食的文化基地。

The Chinese Ethnic Culture Park is China's largest center for displaying the architectures, customs, dances, songs, folk crafts and food of all ethnic groups.

中華民族園。中国各民族の伝統建築、民俗風情、歌と踊り、民間工芸品と美食の展示を主とするパークとしては、ここはトップ。

중화민족원은 중국에서 최대 민족전통건축을 전시하는 곳이며 민속풍습, 가무표현, 공예제작과 미식문화의를 전시하는 기지이다.

Le Jardin des nationalités de Chine sert à présenter l'architecture traditionnelle, les coutumes, les chants, les danses, l'art artisanal et la gastronomie des diverses ethnies.

Сад китайских национальностей является крупнейшей культурной базой, где показываются архитектуры, традиции, фольклоры, пение, танцы и готовка блюд разных национальностей в Китае.

Il Parco delle minoranze etniche della Cina costituisce un grande centro culturale che presenta tutti gli stili architettonici tradizionali del vasto territorio cinese, e insieme i costumi, il folclore, spettacoli di canto e danze, l'artigianato e la cultura culinaria delle numerose etnie cinesi.

Der Kulturpark der Nationalitätenpark Chinas liegt an der Minzu-Straße des Stadtbezirkes Chaoyang. Hier kann man nicht nur die Architektur, Sitten und Gebräuche, die Gesangs- und Tanzkunst sowie die Esskultur der Nationalitäten Chinas, sondern auch ihre kunsthandwerkliche Produkte kennenlernen.

Parque Folklórico de China, dedicado a los espectáculos y exhibiciones de danzas, canciones y demás manifestaciones de la cultura y la cocina de las diferentes etnias del país.

世界公园，汇集了世界50个国家110余处人文自然景观，是亚洲最大的大比例微缩主题公园之一。

Beijing World Park contains miniatures of 110 renowned manmade and natural attractions of 50 countries across the world, making it one of the largest miniature theme parks in Asia.

世界公園。世界50あまりの国家の110ヶ所の自然と人文景観を再現するパークである。アジア最大のミニチュア・パークの1つ。

세계공원은 세계50여개 국가의 110곳의 인문자연경관을 집중시킨 아시아 최대 비례로 축소한 테마공원의 하나이다.

Le Parc du Monde où sont réunis plus de 110 sites naturels et artificiels est un des plus grands parcs en Asie avec pour thème des modèles réduits à grande échelle de sites célèbres au monde.

Der Weltpark liegt bei Dabaotai des Stadtbezirkes Fengtai und wurde zwischen 1991 und 1993 angelegt. Hier konzentrieren sich über 110 Minibauwerke aus 50 Staaten.

Al suo interno il Parco del Mondo racchiude le miniature di 110 famose località del mondo di 50 paesi diversi. Il parco è il più grande del suo genere in Asia.

Парк мира является одним из крупнейших в Азии парков с миниатюрными копиями. Здесь сосредоточены миниатюрные копии 110 известных достопримечательностей из 50 стран мира.

El Parque Mundial es el mayor de Asia dedicado al tema de las miniaturas. En él se reúnen más de 110 sitios famosos del mundo de unos 50 países.

北京游乐园位于龙潭湖畔，是集欧美风格和中国园林景观一体的园林式文化游乐场所。

Beijing Amusement Park, by Longtan Lake, is a garden-like entertainment and recreation venue integrating Western and Chinese styles.

北京遊楽園。北京市竜潭湖畔にある。西洋と中国風格の庭園を一体に集めたレクリエーションセンターである

베이징놀이공원은 룽탄호(龍潭湖) 주변에 있는 유럽품격과 중국조경경관을 한몸에 지닌 원림식 문화오락장소이다.

Situé au bord du lac Longtan, le Jardin de divertissement de Beijing est un lieu de distraction combinant les styles européen et américain et les sites jardiniers de Chine.

Der Vergnügungspark Beijings liegt am Ufer des Longtan-Sees des Stadtbezirkes Chongwen und wurde im Jahre 1987 erbaut.

Il Parco dei divertimenti di Pechino, situato nella parte occidentale del Parco Longtanhu, è un luogo ricreativo realizzato con la mescolanza di stile dei giardini occidentali e cinesi.

Пекинский парк аттракционов находится на берегу озера Лунтаньху. Здесь евро-американский колорит гармонично сочетается с китайскими садами.
A la orilla del lago Longtanhu se sitúa el Parque de Recreo de Beijing, un lugar de distracción que combina el estilo europeo y el chino.

石景山游乐园，以格林童话中灰姑娘城堡为中心，构成一个多个童话人物故事的美妙游乐世界。

Shijingshan Amusement Park, with the Cinderella Castle as the center, is a fairyland for people of all ages.

石景山遊楽園。グリーン童話のシンデレラ砦を中心とする子供遊園地である。

스징산(石景山)놀이공원은 그린동화 중의 신데렐라성보를 중심으로 여러 동화인물의 스토리로 만들어진 미묘한 오락세계이다.

Avec le château de la Cendrillon décrit dans le conte de fées de Perrault pour attraction principale, le Jardin de divertissement de Shijingshan constitue un monde merveilleux avec de nombreux personnages de contes de fées.

Der Shijingshan-Vergnügungspark liegt bei Bajiaocun des Stadtbezirkes Shijingshan. Tritt man in diesen Park, fühlt man sich wie in einem Grimm-Märchenland.

Il Parco di divertimenti Shijingshan con il Castello di Cenerentola costituisce un meraviglioso mondo di favole e divertimento molto amato dai bambini.

Шицзиншаньский парк аттракционов является чудесным миром со многими персонажами сказок, центр которого стоит замок Золушки.

Parque de Recreo de Shijingshan, con el Castillo de Cenicienta como centro, forma un mundo de alegría, en el que viven muchos personajes de cuentos infantiles.

图书在版编目（CIP）数据

北京风景／万博艺林图书有限公司编著 . – 北京：外文出版
社，2008
ISBN 978–7–119–05345–5

Ⅰ . 北⋯　Ⅱ . 万⋯　Ⅲ . 北京风景 – 画册　Ⅳ . K928.91
中国版本图书馆 CIP 数据核字（2008）第 053583 号

编　　著：万博艺林图书有限公司
责任编辑：兰佩瑾
摄　　影：张肇基　卞志武　谭　　明
　　　　　王文波　姜景余　武冀平
　　　　　陆　岩　李　江

北京风景

ⓒ　外文出版社

外文出版社出版

（中国北京百万庄大街 24 号）

邮政编码：100037

外文出版社网页：http://www.flp.com.cn

外文出版社电子邮件地址：info@flp.com.cn

sales@flp.com.cn

2008 年 5 月（12 开）第 1 版

2008 年第 1 版第 1 次印刷

（英、汉、法、德、日、俄、意、西、韩）

ISBN 978–7–119–05345–5

06000（平）